DID YOU KNOW THAT...

- *In Japan a business relationship built on friendship and trust is valued more than one depending on the best price.*
- *There are definite rules for presenting your business card.*
- *No is an unacceptable word.*
- *Japanese corporations employ their workers for life.*
- *Your first business strategy should be to have your deadline extended.*
- *Your greatest business mistake is likely to be impatience.*

Let DIANA ROWLAND be your guide to successful negotiation and socializing in Japan. Ms. Rowland, an American, lived in Japan for six years and subsequently worked as the assistant to the president of a Japanese trading company at its California branch. She speaks fluent Japanese and knows firsthand the ways of the Japanese—and the pleasures and pitfalls of negotiating in a culture so very different from our own.

Currently, from her office in San Diego, California, Diana Rowland provides training and consultation for American and Japanese corporations on effective cross-cultural business dealings.

Please turn the page for praise
from the press and
top businessmen alike.

"A must for Americans who have, or hope to have, any business dealings with the Japanese. Carries the American corporate traveler beyond the Japanese office . . . making this the perfect paperback to buy and read now, and take along to Japan someday."
—*Washington Business Journal*

*

"Should be required reading for all American businessmen or students hoping to be successful in their endeavors in Japan."
—*Hawaii Herald*

*

"Concise, organized guide to Japanese rituals and customs observed in business and personal dealings . . . useful for tourists, expats, and business travelers." —*International Living*

*

"Provides a wealth of information of interest to businesspeople."
—*Publishers Weekly*

*

" . . .the most complete guide for businesspeople and visitors that I have ever had the pleasure to read."
—*Thomas P. Henry, V.P.,*
Director International Sales, ALCAS

*

"Ms. Rowland's book is a must for anyone going to negotiate in Japan or being transferred there. I heartily endorse this book and recommend it to anybody having serious intentions of transacting business in Japan." —*Peter A. Guercio, V.P.,*
Pfizer Inc.

*

"Clearly written, well-organized, [and] full of valuable information, it should be must reading for the aspiring international businessperson." —*Kansas City Business Journal*

*

"Ms. Rowland's book about Japanese business etiquette and practice was a pleasant surprise. I found it to be quite accurate, complete and thoroughly organized . . . American business will need this kind of information if the trade opportunities looming on the horizon are to be taken advantage of." —*Hiro Irita, V.P.,*
Japan Travel Bureau, Los Angeles

*

"Overall, I find the book excellent. Well done."
—*Robert Sharp, past president,*
American Chamber of Commerce, Tokyo

*

JAPANESE BUSINESS ETIQUETTE

A Practical Guide to Success with the Japanese

Diana Rowland

WARNER BOOKS

A Warner Communications Company

Warner Books, Inc., 666 Fifth Avenue, New York, N.Y. 10103

 A Warner Communications Company

Printed in the United States of America

First Printing: November 1985
10 9 8 7 6
Book design by H. Roberts Design

Library of Congress Cataloging in Publication Data

Rowland, Diana.
  Japanese business etiquette.

  Bibliography: p. 169
  Includes index.
    1. Business etiquette—Japan.   2. Japan—Social
life and customs—1945–   3. Corporate culture—
Japan.   4. Negotiation in business—Japan.   I. Title.
HF5387.R68   1985   395′.52′0952   85-11496
0-446-38943-9 (U.S.A.)

To Mr. Seigo Tabata

whose generosity and expertise at blending the best
of East and West were a constant source of inspiration

Contents

Introduction

I went to Japan on a lark. That was in 1971. From the start I was fascinated by the rich culture and rigid rules, and somehow, with amazing ease, I was able to fit in. I never found the Japanese behavior or way of thinking to be alien for me. It wasn't until my second year that I started to learn Japanese, and it was another year before I became serious about it. Six years passed very rapidly before I came home to the States.

For me, knowledge of the Japanese language was the key to penetrating their business world. I subsequently worked for a Japanese trading company in the United States as an assistant to the president, who of course was Japanese.

Much of this role involved liaison-type interaction with Westerners, and it was disheartening to observe that often even those with the very best intentions inadvertently do things that are highly offensive to the Japanese.

This becomes a critical situation when you consider how important Japan is to the economics of the world. America, for example, imports more from Japan than from any other country, and exports more to Japan than to any save Canada. Yet, we have a startlingly poor track record on the number of successful negotiations, compared to those which must regretfully be filed as enigmatic failures.

In trying to help Westerners avoid such disasters, I found that I had a wealth of experience to fall back on. My years working in Japan at a wide variety of jobs, as well as my studies in traditional

Japanese arts, have given me deep insights into aspects and etiquette of the culture that most foreigners glimpse only from afar.

In addition, my involvement in two close-knit recreational groups, in which I was the only foreigner, proved to be invaluable experiences. In each case, the close bonds formed in the group led me to be accepted virtually as a Japanese, an uncommon opportunity for any foreigner.

The first group spent a year designing and building an immense hot-air dirigible, one of the largest in the world. The second group was my skydiving club. Since I was a novice jumper at that time, failing to understand the language around me or the nonverbal cues being given (or, for that matter, unintentionally offending the wrong person) could quite literally have meant my life.

In both groups, however, I was able to observe and participate in the hierarchical structure and intricate codes of behavior which are a distinction of all Japanese groups and which are so difficult for foreigners to penetrate.

Since coming back from Japan, it has been a disappointment that there is no book I could recommend to help guide my Western friends through this unfamiliar territory of dealing with the Japanese. The Japanese, on the other hand, have numerous books of this sort about the West. They have spent many years studying our customs and our consumers—this undoubtedly contributing to their success in penetrating foreign markets. All of this is what led me to write this book.

One of the dangers of a book that deals with generalities is that it could contribute to a person's tendency to stereotype. The reader must remember at all times that while a Japanese may choose to conform to his society more than would, say, an American, each Japanese is still uniquely his own person. Any generalization is, at best, accurate when applied to a culture and not to an individual. Also, we tend too often to look for behavior we expect, and in doing so we unfortunately miss the cues that point to an atypical character.

This handbook to Japanese customs and etiquette is therefore intended to promote better understanding so that business people and professionals from Western cultures may have a means of interpreting the behavior they observe and a better idea of what is expected of them in return. It certainly is not meant for the reader to "ape" Japanese customs. There will, however, be times when you feel it will be more comfortable for all if you follow the precept of "When in Rome, do as the Romans." The choice in each situation is yours.

Throughout the book I have used masculine pronouns rather than the cumbersome he/she, him/her. Of course I don't think all my readers will be male—after all, *I* wrote the book. However, until we come up with a good neuter pronoun, "he" will have to do.

Leafing through the book, you may come to the conclusion that there are many peculiarities to Japanese etiquette. Transcend if you can the impulse to view them as "alien" customs; your attitude will make all the difference. Try to see things through their eyes. This is the vision that is your key to understanding why the Japanese think and act as they do. If you can comprehend that, you are holding a first-class ticket to a successful visit. The customs and etiquette themselves will fall into place.

In the preparation of this book, I have had much help. My heartfelt thanks go first and foremost to Jan Works and Meg Rowland, for their constant patience, professionalism, and emotional support; to Elmer Luke, my editor at Warner Books, for his continuing encouragement and indispensable expertise; and to Bob Rowland, my brother, for his obsession with electronics, which finally paid off for me with having a computer available when I needed it. Without the help of these people, the completion of this book would have been years down the road.

I would like also to thank Michi Swanson, Tricia Vita, Stella Manuel, and Stephen Benfey—not only for all their help but also for the special memories we share.

In addition, I wish to thank my readers: Kenji Urushihara, Azusa Transport, New York; Hori Irita, vice-president, Japan Travel Bureau, Los Angeles; Bruno Braga, Gosho International, Okinawa; Stephen Benfey, Network, Inc., Tokyo; Junko Jones, Berlitz School of Language, Los Angeles; Dr. Tai K. Oh, business management,

California State University at Fullerton; Glen Alder, Herbert Warren & Associates, Woodland Hills, California; Dr. Jill Kleinberg, research anthropologist, Japan Studies, UCLA; Akio Takanashi, Japan External Trade Organization, Los Angeles; and Rich Kamiyama, general manager, Kinki Nippon, Los Angeles.

—Diana Rowland
February 1985

I

PRELIMINARIES

I
Putting Form and Etiquette
in Perspective

Tokyo. A boardroom. Twenty minutes into a meeting. The Japanese gentlemen seated across the table from you are wearing Western business suits as stylish as your own. They're smoking Kents, and they nod and smile politely as the conversation continues. Two or three of them speak to you in English with ease.

You think to yourself: These are intelligent men, obviously very Westernized, with impeccable manners. You wonder why so many veterans of Japanese dealings warned you of the mine fields of misunderstanding and illogical behavior that awaited you on this, your first business trip to Japan.

It's been a long meeting, and you end it feeling confident about your prospects. But then, weeks go by with no further communication. All your attempts to make an appointment or get phone calls returned are thwarted. Bewildered, you leave Japan and return home with no deal made.

What could the problem be? you wonder. Hadn't they agreed with everything you said? Hadn't you given one of your most aggressive and lucid presentations ever? In fact, you remember that you felt so good at the end of the last meeting that you affectionately patted one of your new Japanese friends on the back. You remember saying to him, "I'm sure you'll decide to go with us—it's a price that can't be beat. You've seen that none of our competitors' products even comes close." And your friend nodded, saying, "Yes, that's true," as his negotiating team had done throughout the discussions.

Weeks later, you finally get an answer—indirectly through a friend: no, they're not interested.

Naturally, you're perplexed. You reassess the negotiations. What signals did you misread? What did you do wrong? How could you have blown it so badly? Were you rude without knowing it?

It is a complicated situation, but it is primarily because the Japanese appear so Westernized that we expect other fundamental similarities in their behavior—similarities that simply don't exist. Of course, Western notions have had a large impact on Japanese culture and no doubt will continue to do so. However, the Japanese have mastered the art of adopting desirable aspects of other cultures without changing their own basic values and customs, much the way an overcoat gives one a different appearance without the garments underneath having been changed.

Japanese manners have long been dictated by a highly evolved system of ethics. For a multitude of reasons, this system endures, working remarkably well within Japanese culture. For many of the same reasons, it behooves anyone having contact with the Japanese to be aware of the form and etiquette that are basic to this system of ethics. The more you know about these implicit rules of behavior, the less likely you are to misrepresent yourself or misunderstand your Japanese associates. The more versed you are in simple customs, the more favorably will you—and what you represent—be viewed. It may be that a small gesture will make a large difference.

The first thing you must realize is that for the Japanese, proper etiquette and form are of paramount importance. In the West, especially in the United States, behavior is guided by an abstract code based loosely on what is generally referred to as the Judeo-Christian ethic. Westerners are disciplined by a moral sense of guilt, and in that context manners become a kind of incidental courtesy.

Japanese culture, on the other hand, has always been obsessed with form and has created a strict code of behavior reinforced by the consequence of severe embarrassment if proper form is not maintained at all times. So important is this sense of form that in past centuries people were regularly beheaded for breaches of etiquette. Unlike the should-dos when in the presence of others that influence Western manners, the Japanese code at one time dictated what a person wore, what and how he ate, what he said in a given situation, and even the position in which he slept.

Comparatively speaking, things have loosened up. Nonetheless, the importance of detailed rules governing a wide range of behavior remains, and many of these specificities of form have spilled over into the business world of modern Japan. How successfully you interact with your Japanese hosts—in social no less than business situations—will depend greatly on how well you understand many of these ideas.

Some of the most important to keep in mind are as follows:

- The Japanese believe that surface harmony must be maintained at all costs.
- In situations of conflict, the Japanese will try to "save face" for themselves and, often, for their adversaries as well.
- The Japanese have a strong aversion to confronting others in open opposition.
- The sense of obligation is a powerful motivator of Japanese behavior.
- The similarity of background and habits shared by the Japanese permits them to understand one another with very little or no verbalization.
- For the Japanese, cooperation among all members of a group takes precedence over individual responsibility, authority, or initiative.
- The Japanese believe that decisions based on logic alone reflect a coldness and insensitivity to human nature.
- The Japanese value harmony above truth. They will not question a situation when questions may create discomfort.

To attempt to explain the Japanese character would take volumes and years of study. That's not the purpose here. My aim is to acquaint you with some of the basics of form that are integral to the Japanese culture, offering at the same time as much insight as feasible in a handbook such as this.

To return to our Tokyo board meeting, if all of you were sitting on *tatami* mats, dressed in kimono, and negotiating in the Japanese language, you would probably conclude that despite outward dissimilarities, people everywhere are indeed the same at heart. It's the point of view of, as the saying goes, where you're coming from. The aura of the Japanese being Western—as opposed to our being Japanese—is what creates much of our false expectations and ensuing confusion.

For the Japanese too, one can imagine moments of uncertainty whether to affect Western behavior. Of course, Japanese who have extensive experience with Westerners might well be attuned to and comfortable with Western patterns of thought and behavior, but it's a never-certain proposition. Thus, the following chapters should be used as a guide to more traditional Japanese customs. The visiting Westerner, however, should remember at all times to be sensitive to social expectations (be it a handshake or a bow) and committed to not causing undue embarrassment either to the Japanese host or to oneself.

2
Making Contact

In Japan, a business relationship that is built on friendship and trust is generally valued more than one that depends on the best price. While this is not entirely foreign to the West, "who you know" takes on new meaning in Japan, especially at the beginning of a business venture.

Connections—perhaps more in Japan than elsewhere—is the name of the game. Connections are critical to getting anything done. In fact, it would be unwise even to consider approaching a Japanese businessman or government official without going through an intermediary for that all-important introduction. Getting one person to introduce you to another prior to a first business meeting is more than a polite custom: it is part of the ethics of Japanese business life. Indeed, going through proper channels is helpful because the Japanese feel honor-bound to welcome anyone who comes prepared with a letter of introduction from a common friend or an important business reference. Often this introduction is done by someone writing a note of endorsement on his business card.

The Introducer

Since the Japanese tend to be wary of anyone who approaches them without a personal introduction, any connection is better than none. Your introducer is called a *shokai-sha.* It is best to choose a *shokai-sha* whose status is respected or to whom the individual you want to meet has a sense of obligation. This may be a superior in the same company, a close family friend or relative, an old schoolmate or professor, an important supplier to his firm, an officer of his company's bank, or a member of one of the associations listed in appendix C. When you have absolutely no other choice, at the very least obtain a letter of introduction from your embassy.

The introducer, or *shokai-sha,* may later act as a mediator, or *chukai-sha,* when the negotiating gets tough. His role as *chukai-sha,* a person who acts as a trusted and respected go-between in business affairs, may play a crucial part in determining the outcome of the negotiations; he can also give you suggestions along the way.

In Japan, banks rather than shareholders are the main source of capital, and the debt/equity ratio of Japanese companies is much higher than that of those in the West. In addition, many companies are tied together in a group united by a bank, which may be intimately involved in the company's decisions. For this reason, bank officers make excellent *shokai-sha* or *chukai-sha.*

Another unusual feature of the Japanese business structure that may be confusing to the uninitiated is the existence of large trading companies, *sogo-shosha.* These trading companies handle much of Japan's trade and generally keep the wheels of commerce well-greased. Although there are thousands of *sogo-shosha* in Japan, fewer than a dozen of the largest of them handle over half of Japan's import/export trade. (See appendix C for more on trading companies.)

Finding out which bank is affiliated with the company you wish to deal with—as well as whether it is tied to a major *sogo-shosha*—is vitally important. This is true especially if the company is associated with one of the powerful industrial/financial groups (for example, Mitsubishi, Mitsui, Sumitomo, Fuji, etc.). The affiliations of various companies and *sogo-shosha* can be found in *The Japan Company Handbook,* published biannually by Toyo Keizai Shimposha; this book can be consulted at Japan External Trade Organization (JETRO) offices and Japanese consulates (see appendix C). For a more extensive look at Japanese business connections, see *Industrial Groupings in Japan* from Dodwell Marketing Consultants, also published biannually.

Someone who has held a government office can be particularly useful to you if dealing with the bureaucracy is likely to be a problem. For this same reason, former government officials are often hired by trading companies.

Shokai-sha can also be hired through accounting and law firms in the West that have branches in Japan.

The first task of the *shokai-sha* should be to sound out the company you wish to approach to see if it is even interested. Otherwise, many frustrating months might pass before that becomes apparent one way or another.

The *shokai-sha* will expect some sort of remuneration for his trouble. This could be direct payment or a piece of the action. A less expensive alternative could be an invitation to your country. Your *shokai-sha* will probably be very satisfied with being escorted and treated to a couple of memorable days at a famous resort.

Who's the Boss?

Even if you manage to get an introduction to the individual who appears, by his title or place on the organization chart, to have the final decision-making responsibility, there is another obstacle to overcome—the *ringi* system of sharing authority. (This is discussed in more detail in chapter 5.)

The group approach to management that is practiced by Japanese companies may be a very democratic system, but it makes it hard to figure out who has ultimate authority. There is no one individual "in charge." Managers share responsibility—the larger the company and the project proposed, the more sections or departments involved. Most likely you will have to meet and deal with all of them to accomplish your objective.

Seniority is key to this aspect of Japanese management. Usually it counts more than leadership ability, although this is slowly changing. The thing to remember is that you must cultivate your connections among a company's middle managers as well as top management, because they too will be involved in the decision-making process and will have influence in shaping the opinions of top management.

Although it may be frustrating to have to establish personal relationships with all the decision makers, in the long run it will be worth the effort. Learn to use the system; get input from all people involved, and revise your proposal to meet their concerns as much as possible.

Help the group to reach a consensus. Change your plan as necessary to enable your supporters to persuade others. Cover all your bases by asking each individual involved how to establish a good relationship with the others. Make sure that you do not create threatening or embarrassing situations that will interfere with a harmonious consensus in your favor.

3
Meeting People

In the sense that they are eager to make friends and create a favorable business climate, the people you meet in Japan are not much different from those you meet anywhere else. It's just that in Japan, as you're finding, unfamiliar customs apply. Because first impressions—in Japan as everywhere else—are important, be prepared to do three things when you first meet the people you've come to Japan to do business with: utter the appropriate greeting, bow, and present your business card.

The Greeting

Traditional introductory greetings are the same whether it is a self-introduction or one made by someone else. Start by saying your name, even if you are repeating what your introducer has said. Then, as you would normally, express some kind of pleasure at the acquaintance. You might say, for example, "I'm Jonathan Smith. It's a pleasure to meet you." Or in Japanese, *"Hajimemashite. Smith Jonathan desu. Dozo yoroshiku."* This translates to: "It's my first time to have the pleasure. I'm Jonathan Smith. Please feel kindly disposed toward me." Even if your Japanese is faulty—or even if these are the only Japanese words you know—having attempted this greeting will be a step in the right direction.

In Japanese, the first of a person's two names is the family name; the second is the given name (what we would ordinarily call our "first" name). When speaking in English, though, give your name in its usual first-name-first order.

Always address or refer to your new acquaintance by his family name or title; then attach the suffix -*san,* as in Tanaka-san or Nakagawa-san. Given names are used only among family members and very close friends. (Of course, a Westernized Japanese might prefer first names, but do not presume.)

The suffix -*san* is the closest equivalent to Mr. or Ms. Because -*san* is an honorific term denoting respect, however, *never* add it after your own name. You'll notice that when the Japanese speak to you, -*san* will always be attached to your name—as in Smith-san.

It is safest to follow the Japanese custom of referring to someone in terms of his position within a group. Common titles include *shacho* (president) or *kacho* (section head).

The Bow

Although handshakes are becoming more common, especially when greeting a Westerner, traditional bows are still the rule. Bows are used for greetings and farewells, for expressing appreciation, for making apologies, and for making requests. Before and after a negotiating session, both parties will bow at least once.

Traditionally a bow is an act of humbling oneself before another, an act of showing respect. It is done by rounding the back slightly as the head is lowered. It can be done when standing or when kneeling in Japanese fashion if one is sitting in a Japanese-style room.

The deeper, more formal bow is used primarily for the initial greetings of the day. You'll see it at formal occasions too. The body is bent at about a thirty-degree angle from the waist. For men, the hands are placed palms down on the thighs, fingers pointing toward the knees. For women, the hands are folded before them as the bow is made.

Deep bows are usually held for about three seconds, but if one party remains bowed, the other should bow again to acknowledge the expression of respect. Be careful not to rise from your bow before the other does. On most occasions, especially when saying good-bye, there will be more than one bow.

If you would like to shake hands, you can initiate this immediately after the bow. It's something the Japanese may now expect. Since it is not a traditional part of their culture, however, it would be unwise to judge a Japanese on the firmness of his handshake in the way we might do in the West. A weak handshake may simply be from lack of practice.

The informal bow—a fifteen-degree angle from the waist with the hands left at the sides—is used throughout the day between people of all ranks. (Women again will cross their hands on their thighs to indicate greater humility.) This type of bow is held for only a second or two.

It would be rude not to return a bow. Be prepared for perhaps a handshake too, but remember that for the Japanese a bow is a cultural way to greet people and to express sincerity and humility. There is no need to feel uncomfortable about bowing. And by bowing, you'll make the Japanese feel more comfortable about you.

The Business Card

Exchange of business cards, known as *meishi,* takes place after a person has introduced himself and bowed. If you are serious about doing business in Japan, you will have come prepared with business cards printed with your name, title, and company in English on one side and in Japanese on the other. This shows your good sense and your cooperative attitude toward Japan, and it lays the groundwork for successful business negotiations. (Refer to appendix A to locate a printer in your area who will print business cards in Japanese.)

When you present your business card (standard size, three-and-a-half by two inches), offer a short bow. Make certain that the Japanese side of your card is facing up so that the recipient can read it without having to turn the card around. Your Japanese counterpart will do the same for you.

After receiving this person's card, take a few seconds to read it. If the person bows at any time during the card exchange—as he is likely to before and after the cards are read and acknowledged—be sure to return the bow. Conversation begins once these formalities are over.

Giving or receiving a card with both hands shows greater humility toward the other person. Keep this in mind when meeting a Japanese of much higher rank than yourself.

For the Japanese, a person's business card is an identifying tool that does far more than conveniently convey a way to get in touch later. The position of the person and the status of the company he works for are vitally important as indicators of how others should comport themselves with him. For example, one might show greater respect to a junior executive of IBM than to a senior executive of a smaller, less powerful company.

Here are two sides of a business card:

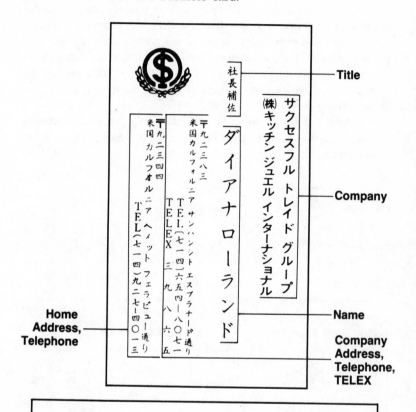

Title

Company

Name

Company Address, Telephone, TELEX

Home Address, Telephone

Successful Trade Group

Diana Rowland

Presidential Assistant

39865 Esplanade Avenue
San Jacinto, California 92383

(714) 654-8071
Telex 705-909

Japanese who do business with foreigners will usually have an English translation on the reverse of their business cards, but the translation may not be exact. Because there is no standard translation of the Japanese titles or positions within and among companies, you may be confused about the rank and management level of the person you have just met. It would therefore be worthwhile to study the Japanese titles—or to have someone interpret them for you.

Below is a list of some typical titles in a Japanese company and their approximate English equivalents, in descending order of importance.

Chairman	kaicho	会　長
President	shacho	社　長
Vice-President	fuku shacho	副社長
Senior (Executive) Managing Director	senmu torishimariyaku	専務取締役
(Executive) Managing Director	jomu torishimariyaku	常務取締役
Director (Supervisor)	torishimariyaku	取締役
Department Head (General Manager)	bucho	部　長
Deputy Department Head (Deputy General Manager)	bucho dairi	部長代理
Section Chief	kacho	課　長

Deputy Section Chief	kacho dairi	課長代理
Chief	shunin or kakaricho	主　任 or 係　長
Staff	ka-in	課　員

It is inexcusable to run out of business cards. Be sure to have plenty on hand, whether you are making calls or receiving visitors. Plan to have at least forty or fifty cards with you if you are attending a large meeting of Japanese businessmen; it is not unusual to exchange cards more than once with the same individuals. Carry your cards in an appropriate, distinctive case, as that will also tell people something about you. And carry your cards with you wherever you go.

The First Meeting

In Japan, the first meeting between representatives of two companies sets the stage for future relations. Here you represent your company as well as yourself when you greet new people. While this is also true in the West, it is more so in Japan, where company affiliation is part of a person's identity. It's important therefore to mention the company you represent soon after formal introductions are made, as well as subsequently whenever you speak to these people on the telephone.

Before the person you're meeting asks why you've come, he will probably want to know details about your company. A common question is how long you've been a part of your company. You, of course, should feel free to ask similar questions.

If there are more than two of you, etiquette requires that the senior person be the spokesman, at least in the introductory stage. You will notice that, among your Japanese counterparts, the boss always assumes that role when subordinates are included; once opening remarks are over, though, he will likely let a middle manager who is more involved in the project take over.

As a status-conscious society, the Japanese feel uncomfortable when someone behaves in a manner or at a level of friendliness not befitting his rank. Such presumption on your part will not reflect well when you meet the company's senior management. You shouldn't be arrogant, but neither should you try to become buddies with those of lower or higher rank than you. Be polite and be formal. Later you can let your Japanese counterparts take the lead in indicating the proper level of informality.

4
Some Basic Cultural Concepts

Negotiating would come next. But, before taking that step, one would be wise to consider a few cultural concepts that are basic to the Japanese. These concepts influence the Japanese character in very real ways—in much the same way as the Western view of individualism and independence affects the way Westerners work and interact with others.

Without understanding the basic concepts that guide a people, one might easily misinterpret signals and find it difficult to decide on a course of action or reaction. What follows, however, is by no means an attempt to theorize on Japanese culture. Rather, it's an attempt to portray the framework within which your business concerns and strategies will have to operate.

Honne and *Tatemae*—Essence and Form

The relationship between *honne,* which can be translated as "substance" or "essence," and *tatemae,* or "form," is like the relationship between the "real" truth and the "public" truth.

Often, in Japan as in the West, there are times when the two truths don't coincide. And often, the difference between the two appears to be two-faced. In Japan, this is an accepted method of maintaining all-important surface harmony. Say, for example, you're working for a company as a translator. Although it's not exactly kosher, you're also doing a little moonlighting on the side.

Your fellow workers know that you're doing it, but they pretend not to know. The fact that they do know is *honne*—their pretense that they don't is *tatemae.*

Another example is someone who has been promoted, regardless of his ability, at the same time as others who joined the company when he did. He now has a title befitting his years of seniority. If there are more-competent men beneath him, the title might simply be an example of *tatemae.* When important decisions must be made, these underlings are likely to be the ones chosen to make them. That's *honne.*

For the Westerner, the feelings of confusion or deception result from failing to recognize the *honne* behind the *tatemae.* Consider it an exercise in perception. If you look carefully, you will see these concepts played out every day, in many situations, among friends and colleagues—and almost always at the bargaining table. The less you talk and the more you watch and listen, the easier it will be for you to perceive the *honne.* As discussed later, *honne* is often conveyed at the middle levels.

Amae—"Sweet Dependence"

Amae has no direct English translation. It has been likened to the indulgent, protective love a mother feels for her baby and the trusting dependence the baby feels in return. It's a relationship quite familiar to the West as well—a relationship regarded as necessary for emotional growth and health. (In fact, the word *amae* derives from the same root as *amai,* which means "sweet.") The difference is that in the West this type of dependence is discouraged as one grows older, whereas in Japan the reverse is true.

Indeed, *amae* and dependence are encouraged to the point that most Japanese will maintain a number of relationships of this kind. In what sociologist Chie Nakane was the first to call the vertical society of Japan, many binding relationships are formed between superior and inferior—as opposed to a horizontal society, where most of the closest relationships occur between equals. Because of Japan's hierarchical social structure, it is easy to determine which role one might assume in an *amae* relationship.

This relationship is often behind the somewhat sweet—although to the Westerner, slightly childish—behavior that Japanese adults occasionally display. It also explains the Japanese mistrust of foreigners, with whom they can have no *amae* relationship. This kind of relationship will almost always be with someone who is inside one of the all-important groups—which could be family, club, company, school, etc.

Without this established relationship, a Japanese person cannot trust another to indulge his weaknesses and protect him from embarrassment or loss of face. He must practice restraint and erect barriers to protect himself, because without an *amae* relationship one cannot predict how the other person will behave.

Imagine you are a Japanese with a good *amae* relationship with your boss. Let's say you drive him to the airport and you have his credit card to purchase gas. Driving back to the city, you pass an expensive restaurant you've always wanted to go to. You indulge yourself. When you see your boss next, or the subject comes up, you say in your best pampered-child voice (it doesn't work saying it in an adult voice), "Oh, boss, I've gone by that place so often. I've *always* wanted to eat there. I just *couldn't* resist. You understand." And your boss would probably be pleased. (To understand why, you may have to imagine this being done to you by someone you enjoy having dependent on you, probably someone outside of a business relationship.) In extreme situations such as the one described, other Japanese would probably accuse this person of being too dependent. Nevertheless, this kind of *amae* relationship is not uncommon and is mutually gratifying to the parties involved.

Oyabun-Kobun—Master-Apprentice

The *oyabun-kobun* relationship has its legacy from the Japanese feudal age (1185–1868). The terms have their roots in *oya*, which literally means "parent," and *ko*, which means "child," but *oyabun-kobun* is used to describe the master-apprentice or teacher-student relationship.

In feudal days, one's boss played a kind of godfather role, and employer and employee were connected in an *amae*-type relationship that extended to their respective families. In today's corporate world, *oyabun-kobun* no longer connotes such a relationship (the term now commonly refers to the leader-follower relationship in gangs), but it persists still in the Japanese image of the ideal corporate environment as one where employees and their families are tied to a paternalistic employer who sees to their every need in return for their undying loyalty.

Sempai-Kohai—Senior-Junior

Sempai ("senior") and *kohai* ("junior") are terms that represent another traditional vertical Japanese relationship. The *sempai* is someone who has seniority, usually because he entered the company (or school, club, organization, etc.) before the *kohai* did. The relationship carries strong bonds of obligation that can last a lifetime, even if it originated in a college judo club.

The *sempai* often acts as a mentor. It is an *amae* relationship in which the *sempai* indulges the inexperience of the *kohai*, and in turn the *kohai* compensates for the weaknesses of the *sempai* (which, because of their *amae* relationship, the *sempai* will not mind revealing). Like the *oyabun-kobun* relationship, this is one in which the success or failure of each party directly affects the other.

Within and Without the Group

A great deal of obligation comes with all the relationships described in this chapter, obligation of a magnitude that can never be repaid and is therefore very binding. Normally a Japanese will feel compelled to try to repay each favor received from equals, neighbors, and strangers; however, in the *amae* relationships described here, personal repayment is of a more subtle and complex nature, and equal reciprocation is neither expected nor possible.

Within the groups to which a Japanese belongs, there is a rigidly prescribed set of manners that one must follow. The closest circle is one's family and friends; the most remote is made up of those people one meets on a regular basis or for a specific purpose.

Outside these circles, however, rules of conduct are not delineated, and this is where Japanese etiquette goes out the window. It may surprise the visitor to observe Japanese who normally have impeccable manners behaving in a less than exemplary fashion. This is especially true when anonymity is certain, such as in a crowd when blatant pushing or shoving is not uncommon and simple courtesies are sometimes forgotten. Don't assume that this rudeness is directed at you because you're a foreigner, although at times it will seem that way. It's likely that you haven't been singled out; you'll notice that shoving can be quite indiscriminate.

In these circumstances, one has no formalized relationship with other people—not even the casual one between a storekeeper and customer—and therefore there is no prescribed way to behave.

II

NEGOTIATING

5
Negotiating with Japanese Ground Rules

When at last you sit down at the bargaining table with the Japanese, etiquette becomes a bit more complex than in the situations described thus far. A specific set of social factors comes into play. Gear your expectations to match what is likely to happen throughout the negotiating process; this will minimize your frustrations later on.

For starters, be prepared to exercise an extra degree of patience; you're going to need it. There are three important reasons why:

- Every stage of the negotiating process will take appreciably longer than you are accustomed to.
- You will need more people on your negotiating team than usual.
- You won't know exactly where you stand until the contract is signed.

Time to Get Acquainted

When setting up business connections, the Japanese businessman's first concern is to develop a friendly relationship. This takes time. At this early stage, there may even be several meetings at which no business is discussed at all. Don't try to rush things or get things moving. Let your Japanese counterparts initiate the business discussion, unless it was you whom they approached for the transaction at hand. The one being pursued, of course, has the upper hand, in which case one can initiate any discussion one wishes. The usual general topics of conversation—the weather, mutual friends, your impressions of Japan, your flight over, hobbies, golf and other sports—are good starters that help put people at ease. Sharing personal things, such as wallet photos of your children, conveys a sense of closeness and familiarity. You will want to create the most amicable atmosphere possible.

Don't feel that you have to fill every silence or lapse in the conversation, however. In Japan, much of "feeling a person out" is nonverbal. Don't be afraid to be silent.

Since relationships in Japan are conceived of ideally as long-term, they carry with them a great deal of personal obligation and are entered into consciously and cautiously. The Japanese will make sure that new business relationships evolve according to customary rituals. To them, the established friendships and harmonious atmosphere of these initial meetings are more important for the moment than the potential terms of the business deal. The stage that you set now can have a great effect on how negotiations go later.

Decision by Group

The Japanese practice of sharing the responsibility for decision making is another reason why the negotiating process takes so long. Although some new companies are headed by founder-presidents who have total decision-making authority, the traditional sharing of the decision-making process is much more common.

A business proposal is usually initiated within a Japanese company at the middle or lower levels of management. It takes the form of a *ringi-sho,* a written proposal that is circulated laterally and then upward. Each person who sees it affixes his personal seal of approval.

This process is called *ringi-seido,* or "request for decision system." It emphasizes the importance the Japanese place on group decisions. It also takes a lot of time. This is mainly because a great deal of informal discussion will have taken place before the *ringi-sho* is even drawn up.

In negotiations it means you will have to win the confidence of the entire group, not just one person—which also means you will need to be more than usually patient. In the end, however, the decision can be implemented quickly and with full cooperation because it already has unanimous support.

The Negotiating Team

In the West there is a propensity for "going it alone." A certain amount of prestige is associated with negotiating a good contract single-handedly. This Superman complex, however, can put you at a great disadvantage in negotiations with the Japanese.

The Japanese negotiating team is likely to include an interpreter, a go-between, the chief executive officer (present only during formalities), middle managers to sanction decisions, operational staff to do the bargaining, and possibly financial and technical experts as well. In addition, there will usually be someone whose main responsibilities are to listen, to watch for nonverbal clues, and to run errands.

A single Westerner cannot adequately fill all these roles. You should have your own interpreter who, in addition to presenting your case better, can be a good source of feedback. You should also have other assistants.

Assistants not only add prestige to your team, they complement the Japanese operational staff who are the real negotiators on the other team. More important, the most valuable channels of communication between the two negotiating teams are informal ones between the lower-level members of each. When problems arise that would be thought to disrupt harmony if revealed at higher levels, they can often be resolved in explicit conversation between these lower-level members over an after-work drink. The real truth—*honne*—can then be shared. It's critical that a trusting relationship be established at this level early on.

It is also an excellent idea to have someone just to watch and listen. This observer can, for example, count the number of times the other side brings up a subject—a good indicator of priorities.

You might also want to bring appropriate specialists along, but leave the lawyers out. The Japanese view lawyers as a sure sign of lack of trust.

If you are negotiating on your own territory, you can usually find out ahead of time the number and positions of those who are coming; organize your team accordingly. Almost certainly, the Japanese will be calculating the same for a team of Westerners visiting them.

Sincerity or Smokescreen?

The Japanese desire to maintain surface harmony at all costs is a very influential factor in the way negotiations are carried out. It's a harmless enough intention, but it's a fact of Japanese negotiation that has to be grasped.

When sincerity in business negotiations is practiced by both parties, discussions usually proceed openly with minimal misunderstanding. This is true as long as both sides have the same concept of what sincerity means. Not so between East and West.

Sincerity in Western thinking tends to denote keeping the good of the other party in mind. It usually means being totally frank and honest, not deceiving anyone by holding something back. To the Japanese, however, sincerity means keeping the good of the other in mind by not saying anything that would cause him a loss of face in any way. Thus, many essential "truths" may be withheld in order to avoid confrontation or offense to the other party.

Does this translate into dishonesty? Not quite, but be prepared not to be misled.

Points of disagreement may come up, but the Japanese will refer to them vaguely, dealing with them only in a roundabout manner. Candor and frankness about "the way things are" are considered coarse and offensive.

Never Say No

In tandem with the Japanese desire for saving face and maintaining surface harmony is their aversion to the word *no*. A Japanese will usually try to tell you what he thinks you want to hear, etiquette dictating that this is more important than the validity of the statement he makes. To avoid being impolite, his only other recourse would be not to respond at all or to give an evasive response. "It is very difficult" most certainly means "no." (This evasive euphemism, along with others, is discussed in chapter 9.) You might wish to negotiate accordingly.

Keep in mind that a prompt reply—either from you or from the Japanese—is not necessarily expected. Silence is valued over a response that could lead to a loss-of-face argument. Silence is also recommended over compromising when you don't have to. (See chapter 10.)

The Japanese have discovered the Western tendency toward impatience and the Western dislike for silence, and they have learned to take advantage of it. Be aware, then, that an enigmatic silence by your Japanese counterparts may simply be a means of buying time or feeling out the next step; it's not necessarily a rejection of the proposal on the table.

Letting Negotiations Evolve

Especially in preliminary meetings when each side is gathering subtle clues as to where the other side stands, it's wise to be humble, indirect, good-natured, and, most of all, nonthreatening. Suppress any inclination to take charge and get things moving.

Do not simply lay your cards on the table. Play them one at a time. The Japanese may doubt your integrity if you make concessions too soon. Compromises and concessions are usually made at the end of all discussions and only after a break, as opposed to the Western style of negotiating terms one by one. If you can, let your Japanese counterparts initiate the concessions.

When agreements are reached, go over each point to make

sure both sides are agreeing to the same thing. When it is necessary to disagree on something, do so in a disguised fashion. Say "I agree with what you have said for the most part, but I have a few small questions," or "Basically I agree with you, but I must discuss it with my seniors." You may often hear the latter phrase yourself in Japan, since the people you'll be dealing with probably do not have authority to make final decisions.

A common method of avoiding confrontation is to employ the services of a go-between (*chukai-sha*). You can be as frank and direct as you wish with a go-between without risking injury to the other party. Only direct confrontation results in loss of face.

If a major stumbling block is encountered during negotiations, it could well last for several weeks. You have little recourse other than to keep the channels open, especially at the lower levels. A mutual friend or go-between may be able to find out what the problem is and possibly influence things a little, but, if not, be as patient as you can. The best thing to do is simply to set your watch and your expectations on Japanese time. Be flexible. And even if things seem pleasant, don't assume that all is well.

6
Making the Presentation

In most business transactions, it's the buyer, not the seller, who has the upper hand. In Japan, this upper hand translates into a higher status as well. So if you, a Westerner, are trying to sell something to a Japanese company, it behooves you to be more polite, more enthusiastic, more willing to cater to your buyer's every need. You should first find out just what his needs are and appeal to those needs.

When you make your presentation, your buyer will be sizing you up as much as listening to what you say. He will be scrutinizing your character, looking for signs of compatibility and integrity.

Here are some pointers to keep in mind:

- A low-key sales pitch works best. Use persuasion, not pressure. The Japanese will appreciate a step-by-step presentation that allows them to ask questions as you go along.
- Presenting a two-sided argument by mentioning the assets of competing products is one way of demonstrating your honesty and sincerity.
- The profit motive should not be your sole selling point. Keep in mind that business objectives for the Japanese differ from those in the West. The Japanese place as high a priority on things such as steady employment for their people, controlled business growth, and competitive superiority as on profitability.
- Printed materials impress. They give credence to one's

claims—particularly for the Japanese, for whom the printed word is next to truth. Published articles from trade or technical periodicals referencing your company or products thus enhance your credibility. More important, though, the Japanese understand written English better than they do spoken English and will therefore get your point more clearly.

- The use of visual aids and handouts is most appropriate. When communication is taking place in a foreign language, much is lost in the translation process. Trying to grasp meanings from verbal conversation becomes tiresome; visual support of your presentation is a welcome relief. It makes a lasting impression. Also, because verbosity is considered insincere, a picture, "worth a thousand words," is to be preferred.

- It is more than simply polite to show your Japanese counterparts copies of cables and correspondence when communicating with your home office—it is a good idea. This shows your sincerity and respect for them as "partners" in the negotiations.

- The Japanese are more kindly disposed to people who are quiet, warm-hearted, friendly, willing to compromise, and good at listening. They are uncomfortable with people who are loud, aggressive, unpredictable, uncompromising, insensitive, and patronizing.

- Comments that are based on personal interests are poorly received in light of the group identity they practice.

- Direct displays of power are considered distasteful because they usually result in someone's losing face.

- The Japanese are sometimes resentful when a foreign company sends a young businessman as a representative. To them it indicates that the company places little importance on negotiations. To their way of thinking, age and seniority command respect. Indeed, promotion and salary are based on length of service with the Japanese company.

- On the other hand, a high-ranking official taking part in informal negotiations makes them feel undue pressure.

(This is also considered rude.) A combination of middle- and lower-management representatives is best.

- Most large Japanese companies practice lifetime employment. Employees are very loyal to the organization and are well taken care of by it. It is wise to keep this in mind when proposing a deal that would require the hiring of new employees. Management will be hesitant to do so unless they are sure these new employees will be needed for life.

- Human considerations such as many of the above points are very important. Avoid being *rikutsuppoi*—"too logical," which is to say argumentative.

Above all, remember that aggressiveness is disdained. Speak of your needs and of theirs in human terms—it's the soft sell that counts most here. Let the documentation of your product speak for itself.

7
Working the Angles

Power, time, and information, according to Herb Cohen in *You Can Negotiate Anything* (1980), are the three crucial elements of every negotiation. No doubt, these elements apply in Japan as well, but with some variation. Because the Japanese consider themselves poor negotiators in a confrontational way (known also as the Western way), they have learned to manipulate these basic aspects of negotiating to their advantage. Here's how:

Power

As discussed earlier, the Japanese prefer to work as a team rather than individually. The strength of numbers is a powerful tool that the Japanese understand very well. It's something that Westerners doing business in Japan will have to counter in kind.

And, of course, if you are going to Japan to negotiate, the disadvantages of location are obvious. If the option is open to you, invite them to visit outside Japan—to your home base or at least halfway—in Hawaii, for example, or Hong Kong or Guam. If you do go to Japan, meeting in a room you've arranged at your hotel, your branch office, or even a restaurant will help to neutralize their advantage.

On the other hand, appearing to be at a disadvantage can be used to your advantage. It brings down the other side's guard and encourages them to help you by providing information and even advice. In view of such, your asking innocuous questions can procure valuable data and may expose some empty claims.

Time

Whenever the other side knows that your deadline is earlier than theirs, you're at a disadvantage. Since you know that things take longer in Japan, your first strategy should be to extend your deadline.

Never divulge what your deadline really is. Because the length of your hotel reservation will be open knowledge, make your reservation either for much less time than you intend to stay, whereupon you can be nonchalant about postponing your departure as many times as you have to, or make your reservation for much longer than you actually intend to stay.

As your deadline approaches, don't let it show. Be patient. Stay cool and act as if you've got at least as much time as they.

Information

The Japanese will have obtained detailed information about your products, people, business, and reputation. You should obtain the same information about them.

Sources of this kind of information could be the Japan External Trade Organization (JETRO), the Japanese Chamber of Commerce, consultants on Japanese businesses, banks, competitors, or your go-between. *The Japan Company Handbook* (*Kaisha Shikiho*) and the Japanese *Who's Who* (*Jinji Koshinroku* and *Zen Nippon Shinshiroku*) are packed with valuable information. These books are available at many banks, the Chamber of Commerce, and JETRO (see appendix C). The more you know about the other side's goals, priorities, finances, time constraints, and commitments, the better position you'll be in.

While these are all important things to remember in smart negotiating, don't forget what is most critical to the Japanese—an atmosphere of trust. Be as cooperative as you can possibly be in order to win their trust. Provide thorough documentation and answer all questions completely.

If you are concerned about piracy, have your product patented or trademarked in Japan. If your prospective customer asks for blueprints that you don't feel comfortable sharing, tell him they are classified. As anywhere in the world, one must be wary of con men.

Throughout the negotiating process, remember that friendliness and effusive politeness are just that. Don't read into them friendship or a deeper respect, which might not be there. Play by *their* rules. Be formal, polite, humble—but be shrewd.

8
Closing the Deal

There will come a time toward the end of negotiations when both sides will have to whittle down their demands and desires. Concessions will have to be made to reach a workable agreement.

Your Japanese counterparts will want to save face for both sides by not letting it appear that either was forced into a compromise, so avoid using a tit-for-tat approach. Subtle bending on both sides will yield the most desirable results. You can offer your own concessions, but don't suggest what theirs should be. Let them come up with their own.

If at this time you feel you are not getting what you need, then it's time to use your go-between—but do so discreetly. If you don't have a mediator, you have no recourse other than to make gentle suggestions. At the end of a meeting, for example, you might subtly allude to what you desire, prefacing it with "you might want to consider . . ." In any case, let it appear that they came up with the idea themselves.

The Westerner's greatest mistake is likely to be impatience, especially at times when the Japanese are silent. Do not assume they are rejecting the points under discussion, and don't give away too much just to get the conversation going again. Maybe you will be able to tolerate these silent periods better by imagining they're trying to figure out a way to give in to you without losing face themselves. Perhaps they are. (A friend of mine who is married to a Japanese claims that this advice saved her marriage.)

Another mistake at this point would be to fall for their generous concessions of goodwill and what they will tell you are final offers. These are part of the game and thus are not to be taken too seriously. The Japanese know they are probably not fooling you (and I hope they're not), but it's part of the ritual. You can use these tactics yourself, but don't back the other side into a corner. If you look closely, you'll see that they haven't backed you into one either.

At the end of negotiations, it is not uncommon that they will ask you for what seems an excessive amount of data. From their point of view, they will need a lot of backup to justify the transaction within their company and to save face for all involved, should the venture fail.

Much of this data will also be needed for the Ministry of International Trade and Industry (MITI), which demands copious amounts of detailed information before approving the importation of a new product.

Signing the Contract

When a satisfactory arrangement for both sides has been reached, it's contract time. For the Japanese, the most important step at this stage is the verbal agreement reflected in a written "heads of agreement" statement. In a formal ritual it will be initialed by both sides.

Even at this stage, you can scare them off if you bring out the lawyers. A typical Western-style legal contract is designed mainly for one's own protection. It will make you appear to be an opponent rather than a partner in the deal. To them it indicates your lack of trust.

The Japanese do realize that when dealing with a foreign company they will eventually have to sign a contract. Just remember that they will not take this document as seriously as they take the verbal agreement. The contract should cover the main points but should also leave room for flexibility. Make it more of a statement of intention than a description of minor details. Flexibility allows both sides to cope with changing situations.

The Japanese will want to assure that they have embarked

upon an ongoing harmonious relationship. Probably the most important aspect of their version of a contract is an agreement to renegotiate, should circumstances change. Westerners tend to expend a great deal of energy trying to hold others to contracts even when unforeseeable events make it impossible or unfair to do so. You will be better off at this time if you indicate a willingness to renegotiate points in question.

To the Japanese, a formal ceremony is an important final step in the sealing of a pact. It should be attended by two officials as well as those who participated in the actual negotiations. In Japan there will be many speeches, gifts, and photographs, followed by a magnificent reception. If the signing takes place in your own country, you may be able to get away with an abbreviated version, but some sort of formal ceremony and reception will be necessary.

This should be followed up with a warm letter from those involved. A formal letter of felicitation and optimism should also be sent from your chief executive officer to theirs. This, however, cannot take the place of frequent face-to-face contact.

Backing Out

If at any time you feel you must back out or refuse a deal, it is imperative that in doing so you save face for your counterparts. If you think the real reason for your withdrawal would cause them embarrassment, make some sort of innocuous excuse. Tell them you need more time to consider things, or simply say vaguely, "It seems difficult."

Refusals must be indirect and are best left to a go-between to communicate for you. Just make sure that your go-between is very clear on the reasons why you are backing out.

Following Up

Once an agreement is concluded, a "maintenance" phase must be initiated to make sure that the relationship stays warm and friendly. Do not ignore this last stage.

Send letters of gratitude to everyone who was involved. Include any photographs you may have taken of informal meetings leading up to the successful agreement.

Later on, personal notes from time to time will be required for maintaining a sense of camaraderie. If you lapse into treating your agreement with them as strictly a business relationship, you in turn will be viewed by them as just another foreign company—complete with all the negative connotations that brings.

III

COMMUNICATION

9
The Meaning
Behind the Statement

The theory that language is a reflection of its culture is particularly true in the case of Japan. The Japanese language is exceedingly complex. Thoughts, ideas, and feelings are expressed in a roundabout way, with the speaker always mindful of who his listener is. Politeness permeates the language.

Because Japan was once a stringently stratified society, social status plays a major role in the language. Varying levels of formality are used, depending upon the relationship and the social and professional positions of the conversants. Unless one knows the position of the person to whom he is speaking, this can be problematic. This is the primary reason why *meishi,* those business calling cards, are so essential.

When speaking to a superior, one uses a respectful level of language, referring to oneself with humility. The superior in turn uses an appropriate level of language. Family and close friends use another level of language, while associates of equal status use yet another. Male speech differs from female speech.

Because society places so much importance on the outward appearance of harmony, the language has developed in such a way as to allow very vague forms of expression. The idea is that by not making direct statements, one has a better chance of not offending anyone. In addition to this, the verb is placed at the very end of the sentence. It holds the key to whether all that came before it is positive or negative. This allows the speaker a chance to study his listener's face and end the sentence in the manner he thinks his listener would like to hear. This is not considered insincere, just polite.

Many things are said purely for the sake of etiquette and are not meant to be taken literally. For example, managers may say to those below them, "Do not hesitate to express your own opinion." You may frequently hear, "Please drop by my house anytime." Expressions like these are usually used without any real intent behind them and are matters Westerners know well for themselves. "It was a pleasure to meet you," Westerners say, whether it was or not.

The tradition of self-effacement can also be misleading. Things like "I am not very confident I can do it," "I am the president of a very small company," "I hold a very insignificant position," or "I'm sure I cannot do this job very well," should not be taken literally. Conversely, foreigners should be careful not to brag lest they make their counterparts feel inferior. It's best to avoid remarks such as "I have a beautiful wife" or "I am very proud of . . ."

Do try to hide your skepticism, however, when a company president hands you a profile that claims his company is working toward the betterment of humanity and world peace.

What the Japanese Mean by Yes

The word *hai,* for "yes," can present another dangerous trap. It is often used to let the speaker know that one is listening and understanding, and not necessarily to indicate agreement. Etiquette dictates that the listener continually let the speaker know that he is with him by means of *hai, eeh,* nods, or affirmative sounds. Warning: listen to the full answer before deciding what the person is saying. The initial *yes* may simply mean, "Yes, I've understood what you're saying."

Care must also be taken when asking or answering a negative question. In English we answer *yes* if the answer is affirmative and *no* if it's negative. In Japanese, however, the yes or no response affirms whether the question is correct. Hence, a response to the question, "Aren't you going?" by someone who is not, would be, "Yes" (meaning "Yes, I am not going").

How the Japanese Say No

As mentioned before, the Japanese rarely say no (*iie*) bluntly and directly. They may simply apologize, keep quiet, ask you why you want to know, become vague, or answer with a euphemism for *no*. Following is a list of some polite refusals:

- "I'll check on it and do whatever I can."
- "I'll do my best after I talk with my senior executive."
- "I'll think about it."
- "I'll handle it the best I can."
- "It's very difficult."
- "I'll consider it in a forward-looking manner."
- "I'll make an effort."
- "I'm not sure."

A blunt no seems to the Japanese more as if you are saying "no" to the person himself rather than to his idea, opinion, or request. With this in mind, it's easy to understand why flat denials are considered detrimental to good human relationships. On the other hand, denying a compliment made to oneself is quite all right. In this circumstance, it is considered a proper demonstration of humility and consequently does not threaten good feelings.

Compliments

Compliments of the kind we're accustomed to in the West are not common in Japan. Statements such as "That was a terrific presentation you gave," or "Once again, Mr. Tanaka has given us an outstanding proposal to pursue," will make your Japanese counterparts uncomfortable. These compliments, by their nature, invite comparisons and lower the status of others. Of course, support and encouragement are important, but even so, these should be given to the group as a whole, or, when given to an individual, very subtly.

To give praise with the frequency that Westerners normally do could be considered insincere by the Japanese. Offhanded comments on someone's appearance, for example, make the recipient uneasy.

A professional would probably not welcome a compliment regarding an expected accomplishment in his field. It's something like implying that he had done well in spite of no talent or pride in his work. This is especially true if the person is a superior; it indicates that you are evaluating him. It would be better to say something like "I learned a great deal from your book," or "I would like my people to hear your ideas," rather than "Your book was a masterpiece, Professor Yamada."

Praise in Japan is often nonverbal, but when spoken it is more indirect and modest than in the West. For example, the giver of the compliment in Japan will frequently express his or her own limitations rather than say anything directly aggrandizing to the other person. Another way is to express a compliment in the form of gratitude. One might say, "Your husband is an inspiration to me," rather than "Your husband is a very brilliant man." Lavish praise of any sort is considered insincere.

The Western habit of receiving a compliment with "Thank you, I like it too," is particularly offensive. From childhood the Japanese are taught that modesty and self-deprecation are highly admirable qualities. Therefore, embarrassment is a common reaction to compliments. Remaining silent, smiling, or denying the validity of the compliment are the most common responses.

A simple, sincere "Thank you," however, on the part of a Westerner receiving a compliment would probably be well taken by those Japanese who are familiar with Western culture. There is no need to act in a manner that is unnatural to you, but keep your behavior as modest as you comfortably can.

Criticism

By and large, the Japanese are likely to be more sensitive than Westerners to personal criticism, even if they are more passive in their defense of it. At all times it is important that you be conscious of the need to save face for the person with whom you're dealing. The degree of shame a Japanese may experience by face-to-face criticism would probably surprise you. In some extreme cases, it can provoke such reactions as suicide or a lifetime spent seeking revenge.

Here are some ways you can criticize without being overly direct:

- Use a third party to gently convey your criticism.
- Criticize in a humorous or playful manner.
- Stress the desired result.
- Show your dissatisfaction in a nonverbal way (such as silence).
- Encourage the group as a whole. This inspires the strong to help or to compensate for the weak.
- Be grateful and complimentary first, but show some reservation by ending your sentence with "but . . ." Then let the person slowly pull it out of you.
- Be ambiguous. Criticize in general, not specific terms.
- Go out drinking together and bring the matter up in the second or third hour of filling each other's sake cups.

In general, the Japanese don't like evaluations of any kind. As mentioned earlier, evaluations invite comparisons and undermine group harmony. Evaluations also mean being explicit, which could lead to confrontation.

Don't say anything to make one person stand out from the group, and remember that modesty and humility are held in great esteem. These should be your guidelines in dealing with unexpected situations.

One more comment about criticism: If a Japanese complains about a husband or wife, it's likely just a form of self-effacement. If problems really did exist, they probably wouldn't bring them up.

Speeches

Even when introduced by name, a Japanese will usually begin a speech with "As kindly introduced by Mr. So-and-so, I am Such-and-such." He will then proceed to make an apology. He will *not* start off with "a funny thing happened to me on the way here" type of joke. Speeches are very serious matters. People who joke too much, or too soon, are viewed as taking the subject at hand too lightly.

You will find that many company members are loyal to the

point of being almost fanatically devoted. This is reflected in their speeches, which can at times be highly motivational in nature and fervently enthusiastic. Watch for clues on how to respond appropriately.

10
The Nonverbal Statement

No matter the country, what's communicated nonverbally says at least as much as what's communicated verbally. Posture, gesture, facial expression, silence, voice quality, proxemics (interpersonal distance), and dress all convey a message of some kind. Because the most important portion of the conversation is often left unspoken, it becomes the responsibility of the "listener" to pick up on what has been implied or otherwise nonverbally indicated.

This oblique method of communication works well in Japan because Japan, an island country, has always enjoyed racial homogeneity and a common language, religion, and value system. Similar to members of a large family, the Japanese are able, to a great degree, to anticipate the intentions and thoughts of one another. One reason for this may be the need to preserve outward harmony by continually avoiding direct conflict. Because nonverbal cues and responses have a built-in ambiguity, they are less likely to create embarrassment or loss of face than those that are indicated directly.

As a Westerner, you can imagine that the more you understand these nonverbal cues, the greater your potential for discerning what the Japanese are really "saying."

The Role of Silence

In Japan, silence is virtue. It is during silent "meaningful intervals" that the famous belly language of Japan, the sensing of another's thoughts and feelings, goes on. Many Japanese proverbs proclaim the virtues of silence, a common one being, "Those who know do not speak—those who speak do not know." Even in his television commercial, the movie star Toshiro Mifune admonishes: "Men, keep quiet, and drink Sapporo beer!"

Understandably, being too quick to interpret a silent spell can get you into trouble. Besides being a time of "feeling out," silence could indicate a range of things—from comfort to discomfort, from disagreement to pure lack of understanding. Be patient through these periods and try to discern first if people have completely understood what you've said.

Underestimating the Japanese aversion to the word *no* can be another pitfall. It is almost never verbalized, so learn to read the cues. The sound "sahhh," drawn out, or sucking in air through the teeth, usually means difficulty. The person may even say, "It is very difficult." The chances are, for both of these, that the meaning is "impossible." Without paying close attention to these cues, you might miss several crucial steps and go home congratulating yourself on a deal that will never be consummated.

Facial Expressions

The poker face: The classic stoic expression so often seen in Japan is a remnant of the samurai days, when emotional turmoil was never to be displayed on the face.

These days it serves as a buffer, like an invisible protective shield, in a crowded land where physical privacy is hard to come by. It is, of course, used to cover negative emotions as well, since suppression of feelings is still thought to be a virtue.

The smile: Like people everywhere, the Japanese smile and laugh at times of joy. There may be times, however, when you think, What's so funny? There may be nothing funny at all. In fact, something tragic may have just happened. The smile conceals the true anguish of the Japanese and attempts to spare you any sympathetic pain.

Indeed, anytime you hear a nervous laugh or see a smile that you think doesn't belong, it's almost certainly covering some sort of discomfort. At this time, it's best not to push the subject any further. On the other hand, a smile could be concealing some other feeling unknown to you. Until you know the person well, you're safer to avoid reading *anything* into it.

Eye contact: In the West we're taught to look people in the eyes at all times. Averting the eyes in the West often signifies a lack of sincerity or pride. In Japan, however, eye contact with a superior is considered rude. Children are taught to fix their eyes on a superior's throat; so if at first a Japanese seems to be "shifty-eyed," he may simply be showing you respect.

Proxemics

When speaking to one another, the Japanese put more space between themselves than do Westerners—especially in a formal situation. If you trespass this personal territory, you will make your Japanese counterpart feel very uncomfortable. Imagine the amount of space you would normally put between yourself and another businessperson in the West—then double it. If your Japanese counterpart takes a step back, resist the urge to take a step closer.

Touching fellow workers and associates is not common in Japan. Patting someone on the back or putting a friendly arm around him is not done. While there is some touching among close friends and people with whom one spends a lot of time, it's not something you can presume. It's best not to initiate it.

Gestures

Every culture has its own set of gestures and hand signals. Some of the Japanese gestures will be familiar, but have a new set of meanings, so be careful.

A *negative* is indicated by fanning the right hand in front of the face as if waving away flies.

Agreement is shown by nodding. People will nod constantly during a conversation to let the speaker know he is being listened to and understood.

Oneself, or *me,* is indicated by pointing to one's own nose (when Westerners would point to their chests).

Money is represented by forming a circle with the index finger and thumb, similar to our "okay" sign.

A *man* can be symbolized by our "thumbs up" sign. Sticking the little finger straight up refers to a *female.* (These signs can also refer to one's lover.)

Eating is mimed by holding an imaginary bowl in the left hand and making a motion with the right as if shoveling rice into your mouth with chopsticks.

Beckoning someone to you is done European-style, similar to the way Americans wave good-bye, with the palm facing downward.

"Excuse me," used at such times as when walking between or in front of people, or when taking something being offered, is indicated by moving the right hand repeatedly in front of the face as if slicing the air. This gesture is used almost exclusively by men.

Embarrassment (or appropriate *shyness* or *modesty*) is shown by women by covering the mouth. Men in Japan don't concede embarrassment.

In Japan, gestures in general are not as overt or as large as in the West. The axis of a gesture is more likely to be at the wrist than at the elbow or shoulder. It is thought that a mature person should have a subdued style.

Bowing, of course, is important. Besides its functions as discussed earlier, bowing can also be used to get someone's attention when you feel you're being ignored. Anytime you find you have caught someone's eye, bow quickly. Automatic responses will make them bow back, and then etiquette demands they further acknowledge your presence.

Voice, Dress, and Other Nonverbal Statements

There are several things that you, as a Westerner, may have to curb in order to avoid making undesirable statements about yourself. Keep your voice down, as speaking loudly is considered rude and threatening.

In Japan, adults rarely wear bright colors or bold designs. Americans are often thought to be too casual or sloppy. Dress conservatively. Cologne and perfume are not traditionally used; yours could easily be offensive. Chewing gum while speaking, in Japan as in the West, is not to be done.

The Japanese are not a demonstrative people. While some younger people may be observed holding hands, the Japanese you will be dealing with in business will probably feel very uncomfortable if you, say, kiss your wife before she retires to the hotel.

All in all, understanding a language is of major importance, but without understanding the nonverbals, knowledge of language could be useless. It's everything they *didn't* say that in Japan is likely to be crucial. Try to be perceptive, and, above all, don't presume you understand an act or behavior until you're absolutely sure of the meaning.

11
Interpreters

Very few Japanese who have not spent time out of Japan actually speak or understand English, although they will have studied it anywhere from two to ten years. This is because emphasis has been placed on reading and writing and the language was taught by teachers who usually were not English speakers. Consequently, you may be misled into thinking someone understands more than he actually does. When in doubt, write it down.

But the wisest—and certainly the safest—strategy is to use an interpreter. Trying to do any serious negotiating in Japanese is a dangerous proposition. The circumlocutions and polite forms of the language make true understanding very elusive. Furthermore, once a subject has been mentioned, it is rarely restated, even in the form of a pronoun. Unless you are absolutely confident of your ability to speak *and* understand Japanese, you will need an interpreter. Confine your spoken Japanese at the negotiating table to the handful of pertinent phrases you may know to demonstrate your sincerity and goodwill. (See the list of words and phrases in chapter 12.)

Whether you are using a professional interpreter or a bilingual individual within the company you are visiting, you should take steps to ensure that you will be represented as accurately as possible. I once heard a very interesting twenty-minute speech in English make absolutely no sense in the simultaneous Japanese translation, solely because one sentence was left out in the beginning. This wasn't because the translator was incompetent; on the contrary, he was quite capable. It was that too much was said in English before he was given an opportunity to put it into Japanese, and the translator apparently had not been briefed in advance on the main ideas of the talk.

Here is a list of ways to avoid such problems before they happen:

- Request a translator who is familiar with the specific field you're dealing in.
- Speak slowly and distinctly, without using slang, obscure expressions, or superfluous words.
- Brief your translator ahead of time as thoroughly as possible. If you are giving a talk or presentation, give him a copy of it if you have one, and allow him time to question you or refer to a dictionary to clarify unclear terms in advance. If it is not a written talk, try to explain each major point in two different ways—and be sure that one of the ways is free of idiom.
- Avoid asking negative questions. If you are asked one, give a complete-sentence answer, not just a *yes* or a *no.*
- Write down large numbers. In Japanese, numbers above 10,000 are counted in units of ten thousand, as opposed to thousands and millions in English.
- Use short sentences, and don't go on at length without pausing for translation.
- Don't be surprised if your translator takes half or twice the time you do. He may be more to the point, or he may be explaining a foreign concept or custom.
- Do not interrupt your interpreter while he is speaking *or* listening.
- Avoid making assumptions of any kind.
- If your interpreter asks you many questions that seem unwarranted, get a new interpreter.

Whether your interpreter is an actual go-between or not, you may be able to get valuable feedback from him as to how things are coming across or what is required of you at a specific time.

Older interpreters, while possibly not as fluent in English as some younger ones, can lend you credibility and respectability.

However, remember that, whether young or old, your interpreter has an extremely difficult and stressful job. Allow for plenty of breaks, and be understanding of mistakes. The Japanese hold impatient people in low esteem, so, above all, be patient. This will not only help things go smoothly, but will make you look more professional.

Your *shokai-sha* may be able to recommend an interpreter or one may be hired through the Japan Guide Association, Shin-Kokusai Building, Marunouchi 3-chome, Tokyo (telephone number 03-213-2706). Large hotels can also provide you with an interpreter for a fee. Expect to pay two to three hundred dollars per day.

12
Some Essential Expressions

Even if you never learn to speak Japanese, learning just a few critical phrases can make a large difference—both for convenience sake and in the way your Japanese counterparts will view you. Though it's just a token gesture on your part, using these phrases signifies a certain respect for custom and courtesy.

Pronounce your Japanese words correctly. First of all, Japanese pronunciation is very easy; second, people will appreciate your not bastardizing their names.

Phonetics

Unlike English, Japanese is very phonetic, and pronunciation of new words is therefore quite predictable. Note that the pronunciation of a particular vowel or consonant does *not* vary at all from one word to the next.

The most common English spellings of Japanese are from the Hepburn or "Standard" system, and this transliteration is used throughout this book.

Pronunciation is as follows:

A—"ah" as the "a" in f*a*ther
E—"eh" as the "e" in *e*xpect
I—"ee" as the "i" in mach*i*ne
O—"oh" as the "o" in g*o*
U—"oo" as the "u" in J*u*ne

The Japanese "r" is something between an American "l," "r," and "d." It is slightly rolled by bouncing the tongue off the base of the upper teeth (alveolar ridge). This means the Japanese will have a hard time distinguishing between our "r" and "l"—in both hearing and pronouncing it. My last name, for example, ends up sounding something like "Rowrand." Don't be offended by these mistakes. Our rendition of Japanese words is usually much worse.

A "singsongy" style can make it very difficult for the Japanese to understand you. Compared with English, Japanese is spoken very flat, that is, without much rise and fall in the pitch of the voice throughout the sentence. Each syllable should be given equal stress and not accented the way we do. Practice by saying HI-RO-SHI-MA without any variation in the voice, rather than HI-ro-SHI-ma as we normally say, or even Hi-RO-shi-ma as some who know a little Japanese do to try to compensate for an undesirable Western accent.

A Necessary Vocabulary

Below is a short list of words that will come in handy for courtesy and convenience. The list has been pared down to include only those words that, if you know no others, will keep you from appearing utterly barbarian.

ONEGAI SHIMASU (informal: *onegai* or *tanomu*) means, in essence, "I make this request," or, "I'm asking you this favor," or "please" (as in a request: "Beer, please").

YOROSHIKU means something like "I hope for your continued friendship or goodwill." It's also used in "Please say *yoroshiku* to Mr. Tanaka."

YOROSHIKU ONEGAI SHIMASU is a request for a continued friendship and is usually said when first meeting people. It can also appropriately be said at the end of a negotiating session or at the end of a speech to people you hope to be doing business with.

DOZO means "please," as in "Please come in" or "Please go ahead," *not* as in a request.

ARIGATO GOZAIMASU—"Thank you very much."

DO ITASHIMASHITE—"You're welcome."

SUMIMASEN—"Excuse me" or "Thank you" (literally "It is never ending, my indebtedness to you").

GOMEN NASAI—"Excuse me" or "I'm sorry."

O-SAKI NI is said when doing anything before someone else, such as eating or entering an elevator.

ITADAKIMASU literally means "I humbly receive." It is said before starting a meal.

GO CHISO SAMA—"It was a feast" ("Thank you for the meal").

HAI, WAKARIMASU—"Yes, I understand."

IIE, WAKARIMASEN—"No, I don't understand."

CHOTTO MATTE KUDASAI—"Wait a minute, please."

O-TE-ARAI—rest room.

IV

THE SOCIAL SIDE OF BUSINESS

13
Drinking as the Japanese Drink

Social drinking and entertaining play a very large role in Japanese business culture—larger than in most countries. As a nation, Japan spends more money on entertainment than it does on defense or education, despite the fact that the average Japanese citizen has had more formal education than his peers throughout the world.

Western businessmen are not unfamiliar with this social ritual, especially in the form of cocktail parties, but in Japan, not only the protocol but also the institution of drinking is prescribed.

Drinking as Cultural Intermission

For the Japanese male, social drinking is an outlet. At the heart of this ritual is the old inflexible unwritten law that surface harmony must be maintained at all costs. Naturally, this is very stressful, as one must constantly suppress his emotions and opinions for the sake of group harmony.

Intoxication is the time, or state, in which a Japanese can express himself rather freely and with impunity—an opportunity to show his true nature without fear of repercussion. It's like an intermission when the normal restrictive rules of behavior don't apply.

Getting drunk, or at least giving the appearance of it, is not only condoned, it is actually encouraged. The Japanese will then

proceed to sing, laugh, even dance and play in such a totally uninhibited manner that it may at first seem childish to the circum-
spect Western businessman.

By all means, participate as much as possible. Besides the enjoyment of indulging in a type of fun you probably haven't experi-
enced in many years, you will—more importantly—earn the trust
of your companions. This is because they feel that some aspects of
one's true personality and feelings will surface during a friendly
session of drinking camaraderie, establishing deeper understanding and a good basis for friendly business negotiations.

In addition to such uninhibited fun, you may be surprised to
witness other atypical behavior. For example, it would not be unusual to see your associates stray from their normally impeccable
manners and indulge in unruly behavior, uncharacteristic frankness, and complaints about or even to their superiors. Under the
pretense of being drunk, a person can indirectly register griev-
ances that he couldn't normally, but still he must be careful.

At all times remember that this is only the intermission and
that the unwritten rule is that nothing said during this time is to
be taken seriously. However, behavior such as causing another
person to be humiliated is still unacceptable, of course. You will
never see violence in these situations, which is one of the things
that sets them apart from typical Western drinking sessions.

Drinking Etiquette

The indigenous alcoholic beverage of Japan is sake (pronounced sah-kay, not sackee), a rice wine. It is heated gently in a
ceramic vaselike container to about 110–120 degrees Fahrenheit
and then drunk from miniature cups called *sakazuki* or *o-choko.*

As with other things Japanese, there is a strict etiquette to
drinking. The main rules are as follows:

- Never pour your own drink.
- Always lift your cup when someone is pouring for you.
- Never let your neighbor's cup sit empty. You pour for your
  neighbor as he has poured for you.

One of your companions may honor you by presenting you with his empty cup, then filling it for you to drink from. When you have finished, return it and of course fill it for him. You may wish to present your own cup to your host or some other special person. If there is a bowl of water present, the shared cup is rinsed after each use.

Beer is often drunk at the same time as sake; the etiquette for beer is basically the same.

If you cannot tolerate alcohol, sip it lightly after the *kampai,* which is the toast, keeping your glass full most of the way. Keeping your glass as full as possible keeps it from being refilled. A common excuse for not drinking is: "A liver ailment—no alcohol, doctor's orders." A glass turned over means you are through.

The Japanese generally do not invite others to their homes for cocktail parties because their homes are very small. Consequently, social drinking is done in bars, clubs, and cabarets. These are all part of the *mizu shobai,* or water trade, so called because this environment relaxes and cleanses the spirit like water, leaving no trace of tension.

In the clubs, more whiskey than beer or sake is consumed. Most Japanese drink their whiskey "cut" with water—*mizu-wari.* If you prefer your whiskey on the rocks, ask for it *on-za-roku.*

Drinking, however, is *not* the time to discuss business or any other serious matter. It is a time to relax, have fun, and cultivate a friendship and trust, which, as should be clear by now, are one of the foundations for successfully doing business in Japan.

"Singing" Bars

One of the forms of entertainment that has won considerable popularity in recent years is called *karaoke* (*kara* meaning "empty," *oke* meaning "orchestra"). What this amounts to is a way for people to live out, for a few heartfelt minutes, their dreams of being a singer. With the background instrumentation of either a tape recording or a small orchestra (in the posher joints), a patron will stand up and sing, with great feeling, into a microphone. (The lyrics, for those who haven't memorized them, are collected in songbooks that all such establishments have.) It's entertainment for self as well as others. Japanese, whether talented or not, feel no inhibition about crooning away in front of friends and strangers, though most have learned from childhood to sing quite well.

It cannot be overemphasized how participation in activities such as this can later turn out to be a great asset. This is all part of establishing bonds and showing what a good sport you are. The Japanese will undoubtedly know a few enduring Western popular songs: "I Left My Heart in San Francisco," "Diana," and "My Way," for example. The words in their songbooks, however, will most likely be in Japanese, so be prepared with a few verses that you can at least fake.

Karaoke, incidentally, has most recently made its appearance in cars where a portable microphone creates the desired effect.

14
Dining

Most cultures place value on "breaking bread together" to enhance friendships, and business people everywhere pepper their schedules with lunch and dinner engagements. Japan is no exception. In fact, due to its strong emphasis on creating friendly relationships with all business partners, you may find yourself being wined and dined more than once before you even begin preliminary discussions.

Proper table manners are of course essential. Westerners don't warm to foreigners who don't use knives and forks any more than Japanese do to foreigners who won't use chopsticks. And that's the least of it.

Rituals of the Meal

The Japanese take a lot of pride in their traditional meal. Great pains are taken to make every morsel a masterpiece of subtle elegance in both appearance and taste. In like fashion, the etiquette for "receiving the feast" is somewhat involved.

The first thing you will receive is an *o-shibori,* a small damp towel, usually warm or hot, on a boat-shaped tray. This is to cleanse your hands, although men in particular will be seen on less formal occasions refreshing their faces as well. When you are finished, fold the towel and put it back in its container. (Traditional Japanese restaurants do not have napkins.)

A typical meal arrives in a variety of small dishes on a lacquered tray. These dishes are not to be removed from the tray unless you are holding or lifting one of them to your lips. Before beginning to eat, you may say with a little bow, *Itadakimasu,* meaning, "I humbly receive."

In front on the tray will be two covered bowls: rice on the left and soup on the right. Remove the lids (rice with the left hand and soup with the right hand) and place them to the outside of each bowl. The meal may begin with either of these dishes. Nothing should be taken from either of these bowls without picking up the bowl and holding it while you eat from it.

To be perfectly correct, pick up your chopsticks with the right hand palm down, take the tips with the left hand palm up, and then adjust the sticks properly in the right hand. If they come in a paper cover, they are the type that must be separated before using.

Remove the cover of your soup bowl. If the cover won't come off easily, squeeze the sides gently to break the vacuum seal. Then pick up the bowl. Resting it on your left palm and steadying it with your right hand, take a sip from the bowl. Pick out a morsel with your chopsticks and put the bowl back down.

Next, have some rice. Holding the bowl in your left hand, take a small mouthful of rice with your chopsticks and bring it to your mouth. Continuing to hold the rice bowl in your left hand, you may now proceed to eat bit by bit from all the other dishes on the tray, except the pickles. Take a mouthful of rice between bites of the other dishes to cleanse your palate. Often the rice bowl is put down only to pick up the soup, which also should last throughout the meal.

It's likely that *sashimi,* sliced raw fish, will come with this meal. Fish prepared by the Japanese is very fresh and has no fishy odor or taste, but if you find the thought of raw fish unappetizing, the best thing you can do is work on changing your attitude. Put your cultural prejudice aside (you know, many Japanese have a hard time with the thought of eating raw cauliflower), and you may even be pleasantly surprised.

On the plate of fish you will usually find a pile of grated green horseradish and a variety of seaweed. Some or all of the horseradish (*wasabi*) is to be added to the accompanying small dish of soy sauce but start with a small amount, as it's hotter than you might expect. Thoroughly dip the *sashimi* in your soy sauce before eating it, in between bites of rice.

A great deal of importance is placed on rice—the staff of life. Leave a little bit of rice in your bowl to receive more helpings. Only when you have finished your other dishes may you eat the salted pickles with the last of your rice. An empty rice bowl indicates that you have finished your meal.

When you have finished, replace the covers on your soup and rice bowls. The proper way to say "thank you" at the end of a meal is to say with a bow, *"Go chiso sama deshita,"* meaning "It was a feast."

A Caution on Chopsticks

Since you will be eating your meals with chopsticks, it is best if you've spent some time practicing with them. Don't worry if you make a few mistakes—no one will expect you to do every-thing perfectly. The important thing is to stay relaxed. Don't make your hosts uncomfortable by being uncomfortable yourself.

The Japanese themselves adhere to a much more elaborate code of etiquette than is necessary for a foreigner. Just to avoid making some really gross errors, however, here are a few dos and don'ts:

- Never place your chopsticks straight up and down in your rice bowl; this imitates the way an offering to the dead is made.
- Never pour **anything** over your rice (for example, soy sauce or other sauces) except for green tea at the end of the meal if others have done so.
- Never take something off a serving dish with your own chopsticks unless you turn them around and use the large, dull ends. This is done for the sake of sanitation. Also turn your chopsticks around when you are serving food to someone from a serving dish.
- Always use serving chopsticks if they are present.
- Never dally over dishes trying to figure out what's in them. Decide, for the sake of international relations, world peace, and smart business, that you are going to eat whatever it is and then proceed. Don't insult your hosts by saying or im-plying that you didn't like something they served or or-dered for you. (Remember what you think of people who refuse to try different foods in your own home.) Showing genuine interest in the food by wanting to know more about it is, of course, not considered rude.

How to Eat It

One Japanese delicacy that has become fashionable in the West is *sushi.* This is raw fish on little blocks of delicately flavored rice. In *makizushi,* rice and a vegetable or fish are rolled up in a sheet of seaweed, then sliced into pieces.

At a *sushi* bar, the pieces of *sushi* come in pairs. They're served with finely sliced ginger and a small dish of soy sauce. The green horseradish will already have been applied between the fish and the rice. If you want more horseradish, you'll have to ask for it (unlike in Japanese restaurants in the States, where, because of its popularity, extra horseradish is the usual accompaniment). Try your *sushi* before asking for extra horseradish; it may be quite hot enough. A hint: breathe through your mouth to keep the dragon out of your nose.

Sushi may be picked up either with chopsticks or with fingers, then dipped in the soy sauce. Actually, only the fish on top should touch the soy sauce, but as good as your intentions may be, it is all too easy for the rice block to fall apart and end up in the soy sauce. Not to worry: it happens to Japanese too! Put the *sushi* in your mouth with the rice side up and the fish side down, so that the fish is first to touch your tongue.

If you absolutely can't bear raw fish, try *ebi* (shrimp, usually cooked), *tamago* (egg prepared like an omelet), *maguro* (tuna—raw, but it has a mild flavor), *anago* and *unagi* (eel, broiled with a sweet sauce), or *kyuri* (cucumber).

The etiquette of eating Japanese noodles also deserves special mention. There are many varieties of noodles (*soba, udon, somen*) in Japan—hot in a soup, fried, or cold with a broth to dip them in.

Eating noodles with chopsticks is simply a matter of practice. The only trick to it is to keep your chopsticks open around the noodles as you suck them in, keeping them from wrapping around your cheeks if you inhale too fast. Slurp (even if you've spent years trying not to)—in Japan a slurp is a sign of pleasure and appreciation. Besides, sucking in air with the soup as you slurp your noodles allows you to eat them while they're still very hot.

Many restaurants in Japan serve only one kind of food. In other words, you won't be able to get *soba* at a *sushi* shop or *yakitori* (grilled chicken) at a *soba* shop. The plastic models in the display cases outside most restaurants will give you an idea of what kind of food is served there. You can also use these to point out the dish that looks appealing to you if you don't recognize anything you want on the menu.

At the end of a meal, green tea is usually served. This is drunk very hot, without milk or sugar. Cups are usually filled only half to three-quarters full and may have bits of tea leaves at the bottom. Incidentally, if a tea leaf or stem is standing up, it's considered very good luck.

One last menu note: a *teishoku* is a complete meal, as opposed to à la carte, that includes a main dish, soup, rice, and pickles.

Picking Up the Tab

Who pays at a business meal is not dictated by any firm rule. However, if you feel you would like the meal to be your treat, you will probably have to be quick to grab the check before your intended guests do. Snatching the bill before someone else does *is* good etiquette, but the Japanese are quick and can make it difficult for you to pay. A way around this would be to invite your guests to an establishment you frequent and prearrange for the bill to be given directly to you.

If the other person has extended the dinner invitation to you, it's best to let him pay for it. You wouldn't want to inadvertently imply that he can't afford it.

The Japanese will not pore over a check—in fact they may not look at it at all—for it will almost inevitably be correct. (No tipping is required—see chapter 24.)

When in Japan, it's probably safest to ask your host to order for you. If you're entertaining some Japanese guests in your country, you might suggest one of the more expensive steak dishes. This is something they don't get a lot of in Japan, and it lets them know they're free to order a dish of any price they would like. Note, however, that a large steak could be overwhelming for a Japanese not used to eating much meat.

Obviously, there are many Japanese foods we've left out: *sukiyaki, shabu shabu, kushi katsu,* among many others. With these, however, it will be easy enough to follow your host's lead.

15
Visiting the Japanese Home

Japanese homes, by Western standards, are very small. Apartments, especially in the city, are so diminutive that they are almost like closets. Even the Japanese refer to them as rabbit hutches. When the home is a house, any tiny bit of spare ground will have been turned into a miniature garden.

Japanese rarely entertain in their homes because they do not presume their homes worthy of guests. If a foreigner expresses some interest in visiting a Japanese home, however, an invitation might be forthcoming. Note that this is quite an exception to the rule, and you should consider the invitation an honor.

Even if you never visit a Japanese home, you will probably at some point be invited to a traditional Japanese meal (always more expensive) at a restaurant or inn. The etiquette for either the home or the traditional restaurant is basically the same.

Visiting Etiquette

If there is no doorbell affixed to the outside of a house, you should not knock, but open the sliding door and call, *"Gomen kudasai."* Just inside there will be a small vestibule called a *genkan.* Here you should remove any overcoat, hat, or gloves. You must also remove your shoes, but take care not to turn your back on your host while you do it. Immediately step up into the house itself. Do not stand on the *genkan* floor in your stocking feet.

It is customary to bring a gift when visiting someone. Some kind of food delicacy is common and it should be presented immediately. If a maid appears, it may be given to her along with your calling card. Bouquets of flowers are generally reserved for courtship.

After removing your shoes (slip-on shoes, you'll learn, can be a great asset), you will be given a one-size-fits-all-but-not-Westerners pair of slippers in which to walk down the wooden hallways. As you pass the kitchen, be discreet and don't peek in. This is not a room the Japanese are proud of, so, out of courtesy, guests should keep their eyes straight ahead.

When entering the *zashiki* or any other room, be careful not to put your fingers through the thin *shoji* paper. Also, if you're a giant, keep in mind that the doorways are only about six feet high. Remove your slippers before you enter the room, for only bare feet or socks may tread upon *tatami.*

The place nearest the *tokonoma* alcove is reserved for the guest of honor, so you should make an attempt to sit humbly as far away as possible, and move closer only at the insistence of your host. You should kneel Japanese-style, the proper way being with the knees a few inches apart and one big toe over the other. Your host will rescue you soon and insist that you sit comfortably. (Here the gesture of at least trying to sit properly is the point.) This means cross-legged for men in Western dress, and with feet to the side for ladies.

Your Japanese hosts will not burden you with decisions about what you'd like—beer or tea, peanuts or sandwiches. They will simply serve you what they imagine you'd like.

Tatami

Tatami mats are three feet by six feet of tightly woven rice-straw pads about two inches thick. Rooms are built to contain a certain number of these three-by-six-foot mats, and the size of the room is referred to by the number of mats. A four-and-a-half-mat room, for example, would be nine feet by nine feet. Usually a home will have at least two rooms of woven *tatami* mats; a traditional restaurant may, except for the vestibule, be entirely of *tatami*. *Tatami* rooms in both are separated by sliding doors covered with thick, opaque paper in the case of *fusuma*, or thinner rice paper pasted over a wood lattice door in the case of *shoji*. Either of these types of doors may be lifted out of their runners to make one large room.

A large *tatami* room is called a *zashiki*. These rooms traditionally have very little furniture, if any, or ornamentation on the walls. (Western homes, with adornment of every available wall space, are thought by the Japanese to look like museums.) They will, however, almost always have a *tokonoma*, an alcove usually containing a hanging scroll or a picture and a flower arrangement. By the way, the *tokonoma* is reserved for treasured items only and is not a place for personal articles, ashtrays, or beer glasses.

In the middle of the room will be a low table with cushions around it. In winter, a half *tatami* mat is often removed to expose, in traditional homes, a small chamber for hot coals in the floor under the table. This is called a *kotatsu.* The table is then usually replaced with one that has a removable top, allowing a quilt to be placed over it to contain the heat, so that one can dangle his cold feet under the quilt over the coals. With the modern *kotatsu,* however, the coals are dispensed with, the table coming with an electric heating element already attached under the table top.

Note: No shoes *or* slippers are worn on *tatami.*

Thank-Yous

A few days after having been a guest at a Japanese home, you should thank the host or hostess via phone, letter, or a brief visit in which you express gratitude while standing in the entranceway. (Traditionally, if you enter the house, it becomes a formal visit and tea and cakes must be served.)

16
Gift Giving

Gift giving in Japan is an institutionalized custom. Gifts are thought to express one's true heart and to convey feelings such as gratitude and regret better than words. The gift-giving ritual was once very well defined and so important that one member of the family was made responsible for knowing what to give to whom, when, and how it should be wrapped. That is less the case today, though the custom remains a large part of business and social relations.

Traditionally, gifts are not opened in the presence of the giver, but this is sometimes forgone at birthdays and when it comes to Westerners. Your hosts, moreover, will probably expect you to open a gift when you receive it. Don't be surprised, though, if a gift you've given is put aside unopened.

Gifts are presented humbly, often with comments like "This is nothing at all," "A mere trifle," or "An item of no value." To give lavish gifts for display is considered gauche; more important than the price of the gift is its appropriateness and the care with which it was selected. As a sign of respect, gifts are usually given and received with both hands.

After receiving a gift, it is customary to return one (*o-kaeshi*) of equal value in the near future. The Japanese hate to leave the scales unbalanced. For this reason, more than any other, the gift should be in keeping with the occasion.

Business Gifts

When it comes to business gifts, many of the humility rules are thrown out the window. Business gifts are purchased at prestigious department stores where they will be wrapped appropriately with the store's trademark paper. Although everyday products are the most common (whiskey, cooking oil, condiments and other edibles, for example), only those in elaborate gift packages and elegant containers are given as presents. House plants and theater tickets are unusual but nevertheless interesting presents for people who may be getting many duplicates of the ordinary gifts.

O-seibo (year-end) and *o-chugen* (midsummer) (discussions of which follow) are the must-give times for Japanese businessmen. There is an established price one should pay for each corporate level. It's not uncommon for company presidents to give one another gifts worth three or four hundred dollars, or for vice-presidents to be given gifts worth two or three hundred dollars. Middle managers will be given Suntory Old Whiskey, section heads Suntory Reserve, and middle-level executives a more expensive imported scotch or brandy, preferably in a fancy decanter.

Also at this time, junior employees will give gifts to their immediate superiors. Such gifts, however, need not meet the same from-senior-to-his-equal standard. This senior would subsequently give a return gift, *o-kaeshi.*

Besides at *o-seibo* and *o-chugen,* it would be good form to bring something with you on your visits to Japan. These should be items not readily or cheaply available in Japan. Beef, smoked meats, citrus fruits, and cheeses are always welcome gifts, though note that all food products must first have been certified by your country's department of agriculture. Duty-free shops and other enterprises catering to Japanese tourists are good places to look for gifts. Here, the gifts will be packaged appropriately and might even be put on your flight for you.

Other gift possibilities might be a special product of your company, leather goods, semiprecious stones, geodes, local crafts, and California and European wines. If you're giving an item made locally, look for something that symbolizes some desirable aspect of your relationship with the recipient: long objects (noodles were traditionally given to new neighbors, for example), durable objects, nourishing objects, etc. Fans and objects with crane motifs are popular as symbols of good luck. As you get to know the people you are dealing with, a more personal gift can be given—something for their hobby or special interest.

While visiting Japan you will probably receive many little gifts. A warm thank-you note when you return home will suffice.

Favors

It is considered rude to ask for a favor empty-handed, but these gifts should not be thought of as bribes. They should be in keeping with their name, *o-tsukai-mono,* something you can use. However, when dealing with Japanese who are aware that we don't have such elaborate gift-giving customs, it's best to make it clear that the present is in appreciation for the long relationship, lest they mistake it for boodle.

Midsummer and Year-End Gifts

Summer and year-end gift giving is such a long-established custom that for a Japanese to disregard these times would be a terrible breach of etiquette. Fortunately, these coincide with the biannual bonuses, so people have ready cash to buy them.

O-chugen, the midsummer gift custom, originated as consolation for the families of those who had died in the first half of the year. These days it involves everyone, though it still takes place during the two weeks before *o-bon* (mid-July in Tokyo, mid-August in some other regions), which is the holiday for honoring the dead. Traditionally, it was proper to give a fish; but being a rather smelly business, this is no longer practiced. Nowadays imported wine or fruit, tea or coffee sets, kelp, dried goods, vegetable oil, or condiments are appropriate gifts.

O-seibo, the year-end gift giving, is even more widely observed than the midsummer custom. *O-seibo* is given in the first half of December as a token of gratitude for favors and loyalty. Gifts are presented to friends and associates, superiors, teachers, benefactors, and anyone else to whom one feels indebted. Stores and companies often spend exorbitant sums of money to thank clients who have patronized them. As well as imported delicacies, one can give specialty meats, kelp, whiskey, oil, condiments, or dairy products.

During the *o-chugen* and *o-seibo* seasons, department stores open up special sections, sometimes a whole floor, to display their selection of typical gifts for these occasions. This is probably the best place for you to shop. The gift you buy won't be something unusable for the Japanese, and, more important, it will be packaged and wrapped properly.

Congratulatory Gifts

Congratulatory occasions are birthdays (especially at sixty, seventy, seventy-seven, eighty-eight, and ninety-nine years of age), anniversaries, weddings, births, children's festivals, business openings, new homes, promotions, and such accomplishments as when a colleague's child graduates or passes college-entrance exams. Traditionally, fresh fish or dried bonito (*katsuo bushi*) were given at these times, but these days congratulatory gifts are similar to those given at such times in the West. Wedding gifts should be taken to the house where the invitation came from at least two days before the ceremony.

When celebrating special occasions such as weddings, corporate anniversaries, or the opening of a new business, the hosts will usually present the guests with commemorative gifts or mementos. At a wedding, this might be some of the celebration food, but it could also be a lovely and useful item.

Travel Gifts

Souvenirs, *o-miyage,* are bought on trips for family, friends, and co-workers back home. Honeymoon couples will often buy gifts to be presented as *o-kaeshi* upon their return. Thoughtful, inexpensive gifts are usually taken on a trip for people to whom one wants to express gratitude for some kindness.

New Year's Gifts

When calling on close friends to wish them a happy New Year, *o-toshi-dama* will usually be given to the children of the family. This is freshly printed money, *always* in the proper envelopes, one for each child. Before the guests leave, the receiving parents will secretly check the envelopes and give the same amount per child to the visitors' children.

Get-Well Gifts

Calling on someone who is sick or who has had an accident is called *o-mimai.* On these occasions one may take flowers, fruit, or money. Presents are also given when the person recovers from a long illness or convalescence.

Gifts of Sympathy

When notified of a death, one should immediately pay a call to express one's sympathy. An offering of flowers, fruit, vegetables, incense, or money should be brought. On this occasion a return gift could include tea, as tea is given only in times of sorrow.

Wrapping

The Japanese consider unwrapped money to be coarse, so gifts of money are always given enclosed in paper. Special envelopes for special occasions may be purchased at almost any stationery store. It could be very offensive to use the wrong envelope, so make sure you obtain the proper one.

Wrapping nonmoney gifts in the Western fashion is not considered rude, but the traditional Japanese style is always to be preferred. Here is the custom:

Gifts are wrapped in two sheets of white handmade paper. (*Hanshi, nori-ire,* and *hosho* are the best choices of paper.) The right side of the paper is folded over the left so that it reaches the left-hand edge of the top side of the package. This is reversed, however, for unhappy occasions, so be certain you've got it right. The package is then tied with *mizu hiki,* cords made of rolled paper. Gold and silver or red and white cords are used for auspicious occasions, black and white for deaths. They should be tied so that the gold, red, or black is on the right. For weddings and deaths, they should be tied in a square knot, but a bow is fine on all other occasions. A word or two appropriate to the occasion is usually written on the middle top of the package, and a *noshi* (dried abalone, symbolic of the old custom of giving fish) is placed on the top right. Store personnel will be happy to inscribe the package for you if you wish.

What Not to Give

Superstitions die hard, so be aware: gifts that consist of a number of items fewer than ten should be given in odd numbers. Four and nine are avoided on most occasions, as they have homonyms which mean "death" and "suffering." Hospitals in particular avoid these numbers.

Flowers are reserved for courting, illnesses, and deaths.

17
Tea Ceremony

In the course of doing business in Japan, the occasion may arise that you'll be invited to a tea ceremony. This is a very kind invitation indeed; it's not extended to everyone. Regard it as a special honor, and go prepared.

There are many variations—and different levels of formality—to the tea ceremony, but the rules of conduct are basically the same.

The Tea Room

In some cases, the tea room will be in a tea house situated in a garden. Sometimes, it will be attached to a temple.

The tea room is designed with harmony in mind—harmony of the kind that can be found only in the imperfection of nature. An amazing amount of money and care is expended to construct a humble and barren cottage from perfect materials to give the impression of refined simplicity.

Besides the tea room itself, there is a waiting room for the guests, a garden path connecting it to the tea room, and an anteroom for washing the utensils. The door into the tea room is small so that one must crawl through it; the intent is to humble high and low alike.

The Ceremony

Upon receiving an invitation to participate in a tea ceremony, call on the host or hostess about three days in advance to accept and to express thanks. Check to see what you need to bring.

Fifteen or twenty minutes before the designated time, the guests will assemble in the waiting room. If the order is not pre-determined, here they decide on the seating order, beginning with the eldest or highest ranking and ending with someone who is well versed in the ceremony.

The ceremony begins when the host enters, bows silently, then retreats. Always return a bow made to you. Everything that happens from here on out is rigidly set. The guests arrange them-selves in the order that has been decided on. After changing into clean socks and leaving all belongings in the waiting room, take the path through the garden to the tea room.

After cleansing your hands in the provided basin, crawl si-lently through the door, then turn and rearrange your shoes and move them out of the way.

Once in the tea room, a guest should go to the alcove, bow, admire the hanging scroll, and bow again. Approach and appreci-ate the brazier. Be seated out of the way. Seating in the predeter-mined order begins after the last person has entered.

When the host arrives, he or she greets each person individ-ually, then lights incense in the charcoal. The main guest asks on behalf of the others that they be allowed to admire the incense case.

A meal of many small courses follows. For this, adhere to the normal eating etiquette for a Japanese meal. Be sure that you say *"o-saki ni"* anytime you do anything before another guest. Take your cues for what to do from those around you.

When the meal is finished, the guests will retire to a Western-style room or arbor while the host prepares the tea utensils, tidies the room, and exchanges the scroll for a flower arrangement. When he is ready, he will sound a gong or appear and make an-other silent bow. The guests will then go through the ritual en-trance again, this time admiring the flower arrangement. They will stop to look at the kettle, fire, and tea caddy before returning to their seats.

The host returns now and prepares a thick tea with practiced grace and total precision of motion. This thick tea is passed from guest to guest in one big tea bowl. The ritual of drinking is to place the silk cloth, if passed with the bowl, on your left palm, set the bowl on the cloth, and steady it with your right hand. Then with a nod and an *o-saki ni* to the next guest, turn the bowl twice clockwise so that the design is away from you.

You should take three and a half sips, then set it down. With your little cloth, wipe the edge of the bowl where you drank from it, turn it so that the design faces you again, and pass it to the next guest.

When each guest has drunk from it, the bowl is returned to the host, who will pass it back to the guests to examine. The bowls are masterpieces of nonperfection and usually have a history. Be sure to handle everything with two hands. The guests should also inquire about and examine carefully every other utensil that has been used.

Next, a thin tea is usually served along with little cakes. The atmosphere and procedure for this are very much relaxed. Guests are served one at a time but in separate bowls this time. You may sip this in any way you like, but wipe the place you drank from with your thumb and index finger.

When the utensils have been put away and the guests have expressed their gratitude, the ceremony is over. Three or four days later you should send a thank-you note to your host or stop by his house.

The tea ceremony described above is a common one but not by any means the only procedure for a tea ceremony. Dinner may or may not be served. Be cautious about your conduct, but be relaxed, and follow the lead of the other guests. Above all, don't fail to appreciate the simple natural beauty of everything involved.

V

JAPANESE CORPORATE CULTURE

18
The Ways of a Japanese Company

How the operations of Japanese companies differ from those of companies in the West has been the subject of many recent books. Here, however, it's less important to suggest what the West might adopt from Japanese practices than to note how certain significant features influence Japanese dealings with the international business community. These features must be taken into account in any proposal of a Western interest that wishes to do business with the Japanese.

Lifetime Employment

It is a well-known tradition in Japan for large companies and government bureaus to employ their workers for life. Actually, this affects only about a third of the entire work force, but it is generally the top third and is mostly male.

Large companies hire people right out of college into entry-level positions rather than as specialists. They will work in groups, carrying out group assignments under the supervision of a senior. They then move through an automatic system of promotions and pay raises until they retire around age fifty-five or sixty. For this reason, age and seniority are usually synonymous. The Japanese like the security this system offers, as they find that it attracts dedicated workers.

Another type of automatic move within a company is the lateral move—through various departments and even other branch offices every two to five years. This exposes workers to a wide variety of experiences, allowing them to meet many different people and giving them an understanding of how their company functions as a whole. It also permits them to establish valuable contacts with workers in other departments, of whom they can later ask favors.

Of course, not everyone is equal in skill or ambition. But the system of group work assignments and vague job descriptions permits those of greater skill within the group to compensate for those of lesser skill. This is true even if those of lesser skill are theoretically in charge.

Those who make it to the top in Japanese companies are those who have the best interpersonal skills. This is because a top manager is more of a human-relations leader than a decision maker or a goal setter. Top managers in the Japanese system are good listeners and harmonizers. They know how to orchestrate the "right" environment and boost workers' morale.

In the beginning, these managers-to-be are not promoted any more often than other employees, nor do they receive pay raises any faster. As their abilities become apparent, they are given tougher job assignments and put on an elite track that will move them properly through the right departments to prepare them for top management. From middle-level jobs on, differences in speed of promotion slowly begin to appear.

Humanistic Management

Japanese companies are ever conscious that their employees are their lifeblood. For this reason, business leaders tend to look after the physical needs and spiritual growth of their employees much as they would their own children.

Companies offer free lessons of all kinds—in everything from martial arts to flower arranging to tea ceremony—and these are usually well attended by company workers at all levels. Company and group parties are regular events. Accordingly, a Japanese company sometimes seems more like a social club than a business enterprise.

More workers will be employed in a Japanese company than in a comparable American or European company. One reason for this is that Japanese managers believe that their people build their markets. Even Japanese law seems to uphold this by requiring companies to employ people in what would appear to be superfluous positions, such as statutory auditors whose only job is to certify the company's financial statements.

The Work Group

Most assignments are carried out by work groups of about fifteen workers. The group, or *ka*, is headed by a chief called the *kacho*—usually someone around forty years of age who has been with the company for at least fifteen years. Individual roles and assignments to accomplish a project are not well defined within the group. Each group member does whatever is necessary in the way of tasks to complete the project.

During the three to four years a worker may spend in one group before he is rotated into another, that group becomes the focus of his life. He will spend from forty-five to fifty-five hours each week working closely on projects with other group members, with whom he will also spend much of his social life. As always, maintaining harmony in all relationships has primary importance.

Harmony is stressed in Japan, to be sure, but this is primarily at the surface level. As one Japanese scientist working in the United States has described, American companies are like a zoo at feeding time, where all the animals openly fend for themselves and go for the food. Japanese companies, he says, are more like an arboretum where the plants are apparently living together in peaceful harmony above ground, but the unseen roots below the surface are in continual competition, fighting each other for survival.

Project Teams

When special problems arise, project teams consisting of managers and employees from various departments are created, much like a task force. At meetings team members "feel out" one another, hearing everyone's opinion until a consensus is reached. The conclusion is then written up in a *ringi-sho,* which is circulated around the group and then up through the hierarchy for approval.

If the team is initiated by someone in middle or lower management, the meetings often take place informally, sometimes even after work hours.

The "Organic" System

One of the salient differences between Japanese and Western companies is the formalized structure the Japanese have for a "from-bottom-then-upward" method of making proposals and participating in decisions. While the ultimate authority for approving all important and far-reaching measures does of course lie at the top, by and large the system is an "organic" one.

In essence, this organic system means that all levels of company management are involved in the process of proposal initiation and final decision making. One good point about the system is that in the end no single person must take sole responsibility for a mistake or a bad decision. And all share in the success of the enterprise. There has been a complete consensus about the matter throughout the group, from bottom to top as from top to bottom.

The Personal Side of Business

The personal side of Japanese business is of no mean consequence. A great deal of energy is expended in maintaining the relationships upon which companies will depend for many years.

To the Japanese way of thinking, business is more a commitment than a simple transaction. Personal relationships are vital, therefore, in developing the humanistic and emotional ties that ensure that a business relationship will not end as soon as it becomes unprofitable—the way Western business connections often do. Business relationships based on an impersonal profitability are not the Japanese way.

Accordingly, dropping by regularly or calling just to say hello is a common courtesy in Japan. Small gifts are given at special times, and attention is paid to a person's hobbies or particular interests. (Gift giving is discussed more thoroughly in chapter 16.)

Japanese manufacturers go to great lengths to convince everyone important to them—wholesaler, retailer, and consumer—of their commitment to the human aspects of business. This concern should be even more critical in the case of a foreign producer selling products in Japan. In the past, many foreign companies have used the Japanese market for the spot sale of goods, earning a much-deserved, and not well regarded, "here today, gone tomorrow" reputation.

The Detailman's Role

A very important public arm of a Japanese manufacturer is its detail force. These are sales representatives who establish close relationships with both the wholesaler and the retailer.

These sales representatives may visit retailers a couple of times a month, often with the wholesaler's representative. They will solicit frank opinions from both regarding the product in question and its future. They will also offer the retailer merchandising assistance, including suggestions on store layouts and product displays.

For the same purpose, an overseas firm dealing with trading companies in Japan would be well served by setting up a liaison office to represent its interests there. People in this office would be helpful in establishing those critical personal relationships. They could gather market response on products, collect information on new competition, and keep an eye on how well the trading company and wholesaler are handling a product's distribution.

The staff of a branch or large liaison office should not be all Japanese. Keeping some expatriates there is a sign of commitment to the enterprise in Japan. More important than business experience for these people, though, is some expertise in the Japanese language and some knowledge of Japanese customs. These Japanese-speaking foreigners could, in the way the Japanese value, offer those symbolic assurances of commitment to the Japanese market.

19
Working for a Japanese Company—in Japan

If you've taken the step of going to work for a Japanese company in Japan, your job is going to be full of fresh challenges both exciting and frustrating. Whether you're a manager or part of the staff, you'll find that the Japanese colleagues you come into contact with have a remarkable capacity for ambiguity and uncertainty.

One of your first complaints will probably be the lack of a job description. Your job may include many other duties than what you might expect from your title. In fact, it may be quite some time before you have any idea what it is you are supposed to be doing at all. The fact that you may have signed a contract to do a specific job is irrelevant. Patience is advised.

Another area where ambiguity and vagueness prevail is in decision making. It may bother you to find that no one will lay his cards on the table. Such apparent uncertainty, however, is necessary for the proper unfolding of the all-important consensus. If each person reveals his position, then he will feel compelled to defend and stick to his stand, creating a win-or-lose situation.

Harmony and "face" are maintained by a subtle feeling out of the other's position, often one-on-one before the group meets. Vagueness is esteemed, and directness is equated with arrogance.

The Japanese work in an open office environment, having very few private offices. This seems to be predicated on the belief that maintaining group closeness is essential to harmony. People who do not want to join the group are perceived as selfish—

something akin to reading a book in a corner at a party. It's this loyalty to the group that has given Japanese establishments their excellent reputation for service. To perform in a less than desirable way would be letting down the group.

Don't expect your work day necessarily to end at the scheduled time. Most Japanese office workers don't leave before their boss does; if their boss leaves early, they often stay much later. If you encounter this situation and find yourself obligated to do the same, it does no good to get out the rule book. You'll just embarrass your boss, and he'll be more convinced than ever that foreigners can't understand Japanese ways.

If, however, you feel you are being treated unfairly, you should point this out to your boss. Be respectful, be gently forthright, and don't be obnoxious. Probably a one-on-one approach at an informal time would be best. Let him know that you can't be fully productive when your needs aren't being met. If the subject is touchy, get someone to act as a go-between for you.

Keep in mind, though, that while in the United States, there is the saying "The squeaky wheel gets oiled," the Japanese have an equally popular saying that goes "The nail which sticks up gets hit."

Workaholism

Most Westerners consider work to be primarily a means to a financial end. Aside from certain workaholics, most Westerners seem to center their lives around family and friends—not around the work environment.

Japanese workers, on the other hand, don't perceive work as a form of punishment. Indeed, business life is often preferred to home life. A dedication to work that is uncommon in the West seems more the rule than the exception. Consequently, if you refuse to work overtime or if you ask for time off for routine family affairs, you won't create a very good impression. If you decline to go on group trips or drinking outings with co-workers, you'll undermine the solidarity of the work group.

This is not to say that the Japanese are intransigent about

such matters or that to work for a Japanese company is to indenture yourself to it. This is only to say that these customs apply,
and any deviation from them behooves you to acquit yourself in
some compensatory fashion.

What Not to Do

- Don't expect your private affairs to be nobody else's business. Remember that this is a group of tight solidarity.
- Don't slap your co-workers on the back in easy familiarity.
- Don't defend yourself when reprimanded. Your colleagues
  will assume that your intentions were right, even if you
  acted in error. Simply apologize and accept the blame.
- Don't press a colleague or boss to make a decision in public. Don't corner him with "Would you sign here, please."
- Don't laugh at a Japanese to his face, even if you think he
  should recognize that you're laughing with him.
- Don't joke around at work. In Japan there is a time and
  place for everything, and much of the usual joking that
  goes on in Western companies is out-of-place on the job in
  Japan.
- Don't make comments on the physical attributes of female
  employees at work. These comments are not typically
  made in Japan and are also seen as out-of-place.
- Don't ask for a private office.

As a Manager

If you're a manager in a Japanese company, you'll be spending
ninety percent of your time listening and the other ten percent
talking—not the other way around.

In group meetings, listen to everyone else's opinion before
expressing yours. You'll notice how the Japanese avoid open disagreement with one another. When dissension is necessary, they
preface their remarks with buffer phrases such as "I concur
but . . ." or "I agree in principle. . . ." If you think the group is

being manipulated by one person, you can shelve the subject with this handy phrase: *"kangaemasho"* ("let's think about it").

As a manager, you may have to modify the ways in which you are used to communicating with others. Don't send out a lot of memos and ask for memos in return. The Japanese don't regard this type of written correspondence as a valid means of communication. They will, however, pay a lot of attention to what you say. Don't be surprised when people want to discuss points of view with you in private prior to a group meeting.

To exercise your influence in a subtle fashion and to help the group come to a consensus, it will be necessary to spend time with individuals outside the work environment—at lunch or dinner or, most commonly, over a drink. If you ever need to request personal help, it is best done in this way as well.

You will need to take a more personal interest in your workers than you probably would in your own country. Japanese workers usually won't volunteer information on their problems to you, but they will expect you to inquire regularly.

Among the values foreign managers have said they learned from their work experience in Japan are patience, tolerance, tact, sensitivity, thoughtfulness, and a live-and-let-live attitude. It follows, of course, that you will need these qualities to get the most from your experience in Japan.

Allow yourself plenty of time to adapt to your new role—it may take at least a year. Remaining flexible will be your greatest asset in encountering the unfamiliar situations ahead of you. Keep in the front of your mind the Japanese successes and the amazing efficiency with which the Japanese way functions when the whole problem is considered. It will help you to be less judgmental when little differences appear.

At a company party, Japanese managers have been known to slip away early, after having made financial arrangements for the party to continue. The reasoning here is that the party can be more relaxed without the manager there, thus freeing both manager and employees from prescribed roles. If you're a foreign manager in a Japanese company, you might want to do the same.

Salary and Bonuses

In almost all cases, the salary for the Japanese employee is lower than that for an employee in the West for comparable work and responsibility. Your salary is likely to be no exception. The Japanese accept this lower pay for two reasons: first, there is the larger societal benefit that employment is more widespread, and second, if the company makes a profit, there is the benefit of bonuses.

Bonuses are given twice a year—early summer and the big one at the end of the year. It is, in effect, a profit-sharing plan. The bonus an employee receives can be quite substantial. Depending on one's rank and rating, an employee's bonus can be as much as his entire yearly salary.

Of course, bonuses will be smaller in bad times, but all of this is yet another example of the sense of group and group effort and the need, therefore, not to forsake the group.

Greater Benefits

There are many frustrations in working for a Japanese company, but there will also be great benefits to your career. View your career in larger, longer terms. Opportunities for learning and new experiences will be innumerable, to say nothing of individual growth. If you're easily discouraged, or if you want only what's tried and familiar, you'd do better to stay home.

As international business shrinks the world smaller and smaller, companies and executives who don't have a global picture will find themselves left behind. If you've had experience working in another culture, especially one as successful at business as Japan, your worth will be more highly prized.

20
Working for a Japanese Company—in the West

I f you are a Westerner working for a Japanese company located in the West, you're bound to find an East-West blend to the way things are done. The last two chapters on the workings of Japanese companies should give you at least some idea where, for your company, East begins and West ends. But anticipate rough spots—especially in your mind—that will need to be smoothed out.

The number of Japanese managers in your company, and where they are positioned in the organizational structure, will greatly affect how much of a Japanese flavor the company will have. This organizational structure will be determined by the nature of the industry involved. A sales-oriented business, such as the automobile industry, will usually employ more local personnel because contact with customers is a primary activity. A trading company, on the other hand, tends to employ more Japanese because good communication with the home office is essential.

Frustrations

If your main motivation for working for a Japanese company in the West has to do with trying something new and different that might benefit you in the longer term, you're not likely to be disappointed. But if you think working for a Japanese company will mean quick advancement, you're working for the wrong company.

Promotion in a Japanese company comes slow. It's the way things work. Quick advancement, except under extraordinary circumstances, probably won't occur in a Japanese company any more quickly in the West for Westerners than it will in Japan for Japanese.

Westerners will find as well—at least it's been a common complaint of Westerners—that they are essentially barred from promotion to top positions. The Japanese response to this is that few foreigners take the time to learn the Japanese language, which they feel is important for top-level communication. This is a valid point. It's hard to imagine an American company in Japan employing non-English speakers in its highest posts.

Another frustration is that Japanese managers are usually rotated out just when one has gotten to know them. As mentioned before, Japanese companies do this to give their employees a well-rounded background in all aspects of their company. This might work against building strong work relationships, either for you or for the manager, but there's not much one can do to get around it.

Working for a Japanese Manager

It's possible that many little things your Japanese manager does will be misunderstood if you interpret them in terms of your own sense of propriety. Try to be clear on which aspects of a person's behavior are a product of cultural mores before judging too harshly. For example, you may have a manager who seems not to care, or seems aloof because he doesn't relate in the casual and outgoing manner you're accustomed to. You're aware that reserve is a valued characteristic in Japan. But you'll be surprised when he actually shows more interest in your personal problems than a Western manager would, or when he returns from a trip home with personal little presents for everyone in the office.

Consider what would be expected of a Japanese in your position, even though you may not choose to affect that behavior.

Japanese assistant managers, for example, act much like faithful retainers. They will not leave work until their senior does. If their superior is out or in a meeting, the assistant will not even go to lunch until the manager returns. Be aware of such notions your manager may have brought with him to the West.

Loyalty is one of them. If you try to make your Japanese boss look good by giving him credit for things you've done, it will eventually pay off with large dividends later. Learn also how to negate without saying no.

It's possible that the Japanese employees in your company will *always* have lunch together, as though it were some kind of law. This may seem silly or ethnocentric to you, but keep in mind that Americans and other foreign nationals in Japan do the same thing. Any penetration of the group barrier is beneficial. Informal interaction, such as during lunch or after hours, is very important. But go slowly. Too-enthusiastic shows of friendliness are not regarded favorably.

Visiting the Home Office

A company trip to Japan will offer you some unique opportunities. You will have an advantage over other travelers because you are already "in," to a degree, because you work for the same company as most of the Japanese you will meet. For general purposes, however, you are still an outsider like all foreigners and will be treated unfailingly as a guest.

The "office ladies"—whose job, among other things, is to prepare tea and coffee for the men—will probably wait on you hand and foot (whether you're male or female, your guest status requires this treatment). Don't assume, however, that you can feel free to make menial requests of any female there. Asking someone to do an inappropriate job is rude in Japan as well as elsewhere. The answer, though, is not to make your own coffee; you will probably have a young male assigned to take care of you and you can let your needs be known to him.

The Western Businesswoman

If you're a Western woman doing business with the Japanese, it is essential that you view how you are treated with a great deal of open-mindedness and sensitivity. Taking an aggressive stand against time-honored traditions will get you nowhere. In time, the people you are working with will accept you for what you are, but it may be hard for them to overcome the concept that a woman's domain is in the home and that her capabilities are best employed in a supportive role.

If you are the only female at, say, the managerial level, you may find yourself rather isolated in the corporate world. While your Japanese co-workers will become accustomed to your professional contribution, they will be less comfortable with you in social situations. Keep in mind that Japanese men have little or no experience in socializing with women, especially on an equal level. They do not have the custom of dating, and the women they've dealt with in business have usually been in subservient roles. They will have a harder time relating to you if you seem outgoing, overconfident, or aggressive.

If you are meeting Japanese associates with a Western male colleague, the Japanese will probably form a sense of group identity with him and direct most of the conversation his way (he's part of the "male group"). However, there are other group identities that may take precedence, such as "company" or "acquaintance." For example, I recently accompanied my company's comptroller, a Western male, to a Japanese bank we have dealings with. The conversation took place in English. The Japanese banker requested some information of us, but he spent ninety-nine percent of his time making his appeal to me. Knowing that I speak Japanese (despite our speaking in English) placed me, in his mind, in the "Japanese group," and thus he felt I might be more favorably disposed to his wishes. In this case, the "Japanese group" identity was stronger than the "male group."

The point here is that a businesswoman will probably be most effective if she can appear in some way sympathetic to matters Japanese. This will help to disabuse the Japanese of their stereotype of the Western woman as presumptuous and self-righteous.

Being a woman can have its pluses, too. Because foreign women are less intimidating to the Japanese than are foreign men, you can amplify this advantage by becoming more knowledgeable than those around you in Japanese language and culture. You may then find yourself being asked to take control in intercultural encounters that someone of your level would not normally do. Develop whatever assets you have that others around you do not have or do not use.

It will also help you to be sensitive to some of the Japanese priorities that may differ markedly from your own. They may be horrified, for example, if a pregnant woman takes a business trip.

Overall, your situation may be difficult if your goals include large financial rewards or an honest-to-goodness senior title that is not for "face" only. Again, if your primary motivation is less goal-directed than experience-related, satisfaction won't be hard to come by. But be aware that simply because of your gender you will come up against many walls, but these walls will not be insurmountable.

If you are an executive secretary or administrative assistant to a Japanese man, you may have to "train" your boss in how and how not to utilize you. In Japan there are few people in such roles. Women primarily do clerical work. Therefore, your boss may unwittingly make inappropriate requests, such as for photocopying, even if that is someone else's job. Unaggressively help him to understand your role.

Benefits

A friend of mine who works for a major Japanese trading company feels that his greatest benefit is the on-the-job training. Being trained as a generalist in a large, diversified company gives one experience and knowledge that isn't ordinarily available, even in an MBA program. Others say the experience gives them security.

The primary advantage, however, is the opportunity to get exposure to another culture. These days, an aspiring business person cannot afford not to be international. For that matter, it will soon be necessary for everyone to have some intercultural experience to break down prejudices, identify stereotyping, and give Westerners perspective on their own cultural limitations. Without the tools to deal with this, we will find we're just butting heads with people we don't understand in a swiftly shrinking world.

VI

AFTER
BUSINESS
HOURS

21
Out on One's Own

With business in Japan done for the day, you may want to do some exploring about town on your own. In play as in work, Japan differs a great deal from the West—so, if you're adventurous, there's much that can be interesting or fun. Don't enter a place without *some* awareness ahead of time, however; if you're totally unprepared, it could turn into a costly, if not embarrassing, evening.

Coffee Shops

Coffee shops, or *kissaten,* are everywhere. They are the most popular, most casual of the common meeting places. These coffee shops offer a selection of coffees from dozens of places throughout the world, and some include alcoholic beverages and a modest menu. The coffee is ground fresh and prepared before you; it has a wonderful rich flavor, but by American standards it is strong, expensive, and does *not* come with free refills.

Some *kissaten* turn into what is called *sunakku,* a snack shop, at night and stay open until all hours. These are distinguishable by the bottles of whiskey visible behind the bar.

Since there are so many *kissaten,* many have features to make them unique. Often this takes the form of a kind of music (jazz, classical, rock) or distinctive theme (art or period or foreign land). Some are furnished with unusual decor; some have underdressed or stylishly dressed waitresses. There are some that encourage single foreigners to give their Japanese patrons an opportunity to practice English, and others that simply give foreigners a chance to meet one another. These are sometimes called "conversation lounges." For specific names and locations, pick up a copy of *Tokyo Journal,* an English-language magazine that can be purchased at book stores, hotels, airports, and numerous other places catering to foreigners. Conversation lounges can also be places to find someone to go dancing with, since many discos expect you to come as a couple.

Kissaten are excellent places for conducting business, meeting friends, getting out of the hustle and bustle, or being alone.

Drinking Establishments

There are hundreds of thousands of night spots in Tokyo alone. They range from local pubs to *karaoke* ("singing" bars) (see chapter 13) to high-class cabarets and nightclubs—including clubs with exclusively male hosts catering to women and clubs that feature only Caucasian hostesses. In Tokyo, the best, and most expensive, of these night spots are found in the Ginza. Akasaka, Shinjuku, Shibuya, and Ikebukuro have lots of fine, more moderately priced places; Asakusa has less-expensive places. Roppongi is fairly new as an entertainment district and attracts a younger, more international clientele.

At many clubs it is understood that hostesses come with the drinks. If you do not request a particular hostess, the next in line will be assigned to you—often one for each person at the table, but sometimes more and sometimes less.

These hostesses act as modern-day *geisha,* pouring drinks for the men, smiling, listening, teasing, and, in general, getting everyone to loosen up. The patron is expected to buy drinks for these hostesses, but in addition he is charged by the hour for each hostess. This can get very expensive, as the hostesses may be called away to another table and then end up playing a version of musical tables. You, of course, are required to pay the basic fee for each one who shares a bit of her company with you.

A well-known customer will be granted "signing privileges" in lieu of on-the-spot payment. Having this privilege in a number of expensive clubs is a must for properly impressing business clients.

One may have to pay more if a hostess is requested by name. This often translates into improved service—though service is almost always good—and in the presence of others gives one status.

A *nomiya* is something like a neighborhood pub. There are no hostesses, although some *nomiya* have women tending bar who will join customers if they're not busy. Many *nomiya* have a red lantern out front and are thus called *akachochin.* These establishments tend not to be expensive, but if there are no prices posted in the window or on a placard outside, be forewarned.

Whether at a nightclub or a *nomiya,* one can buy a bottle of scotch or brandy, write one's name on it, and have it kept there. In fact, it is somewhat of a status symbol to have bottles at a number of exclusive clubs. Each time you visit these places, your bottle will be produced along with glasses, ice, little bottles of water, and snacks. There is a fee for the service and the snacks.

Watch Your Wallet

Unlike many places in the world, "watching your wallet" in Japan does not mean you need fear being robbed. Japan is—and I think few would differ with me—the safest country in the world. The Japanese, in fact, will knock themselves out trying to return a wallet you left in a bar, taxi, or train. So the warning here applies to certain establishments that have absolutely astronomical prices (such as two or three hundred dollars for a scotch and soda) that you must be careful you don't naïvely wander into.

The reason why places can get away with charging such exorbitant prices is that many businessmen are on very generous expense accounts. The government allows these extravagant tax write-offs because it assumes that much entertaining must take place before relationships are cemented. The businessmen are eager to use up their allotted amount so that it isn't cut back the following month.

In addition to the already outrageous prices, many establishments will tack extra little charges on the bills of nonregular guests. It's best to go with a well-known customer, or at least with a letter of introduction. The Japanese themselves rarely walk in cold off the street.

Checking out a club *before* you go in could indeed save you a lot of money and some embarrassment.

22
Love and Sex
in Japan

The Japanese attitude toward sex is quite matter-of-fact, unlike in the West where sex is laden with overtones of morality. In Japan sex is simply considered one of the more pleasurable necessities of life. This, in one clean sweep, removes many of the taboos Westerners have grown accustomed to when it comes to sex.

Sex in Japan is also not as strongly associated with love as it is in Western culture; it's seen as having more to do with desire. While sex fulfills certain urges and marriage fulfills the obligation to perpetuate the family name, love is often viewed as the cause of pain and heartache.

Traditionally, marriages were contracted into. They were to fulfill duty (about half of the marriages today are still arranged)—not to be the only means of satisfying sexual needs. Extramarital relationships, therefore, escaped moral censorship. But, as with everything, there has always been a double standard. As long as a man had the wherewithal to do so, he was perfectly free to keep a mistress (or two) or to seek sexual pleasure any way he chose. A mistress, in fact, contributed to his esteem. Women, however, were expected to toe the line of marriage. Even here, though, as long as an affair did not endanger the husband's reputation or "face," extramarital relations were more or less accepted (at least at the highest and the lowest levels of society). For the most part, all these attitudes still apply today.

Geisha

When Westerners think of Japan, more often than not they think of *geisha*—mannered women in white face, wig, and formal kimono. Literally, *geisha* (pronounced gay-sha) translates into "one who is versed in the arts." A *geisha* works as a hostess and entertainer for small parties or for individuals. She pours sake, sings, dances, plays classical musical instruments, and gets her clients to enjoy themselves by engaging them in witty conversation, teasing, and playing games. The cost to the customer for an evening at a restaurant where *geisha* entertain is exceedingly high.

The *geisha* makes money for herself in the form of tips (this being the only instance in which a tip is appropriate), but this money is usually reserved for the purchase of kimono. The actual fees of the evening's entertainment are paid to the *geisha* house.

Geisha are not prostitutes. Most have lovers or patrons who help to look after their welfare. Sleeping with the men they entertain is not as frequent or as important as the *geisha*'s role in breaking down the hard shell of Japanese reserve and in performing classical music and dance.

Originally *geisha* often came from poor families who needed to "sell" their daughters in order to survive. Upon signing a contract, parents or guardians were given a sum of money depending on the length of indenture and the girl's personal attributes. Today, young girls enter the *geisha* profession of their own free will.

A girl enters a *geisha* house by age twelve and spends many hard years of apprenticeship, not only attending lessons in music and dance but doing physical labor as well. By mid-teens she is a half-*geisha* and can accompany older *geisha* to parties at restaurants where they will entertain. After a few more years of apprenticeship and after an examination given by the *geisha* headquarters, the girl's house madam, and her music teachers, the girl becomes a full-fledged *geisha*.

Today the *geisha* profession has greatly declined. The number of *geisha* has dropped below seventy-five thousand, their function having been taken over by bar hostesses. What these hostesses in nightclubs and cabarets have to offer instead is less personal, nontraditional, but comparatively cheaper Western-style entertainment.

Bar Hostesses

There are estimated to be well over half a million bar hostesses in Japan. As with *geisha,* it would be erroneous to assume that they are prostitutes. Many are married or living with a boyfriend, while others just simply "aren't that kind of woman," even though their job requires they give the impression that they are. The fact of the matter is that the job pays very well—better than most jobs a woman in Japan can find.

The club or hostess will sometimes accept the liability of a customer's bill, in effect giving him credit privileges. A hostess may choose to do this because she can tack on a substantial extra fee for allowing the privilege. Securing that money, however, would then be her responsibility, and sometimes the club will insist that she deposit a large sum of her own money before she can bestow such a privilege on a customer.

There are plenty of hostesses, though, who are willing to sell their pleasures, and still others who would honestly opt to spend more time with a man because they like him. (If you want a date with one of these women, you might offer to escort her to a restaurant or *kissaten* directly from work when she's through.)

One breach of etiquette that foreigners frequently make is to bring these newfound liaisons to various social events connected with business or business associates. This is not to be done.

Gay Life

Homosexuality in Japan has not the stigma it has in the West, even as homosexuals in Japan are not "out" as they are in large

American cities. In Tokyo there are numerous gay bars in the Shinjuku 2-chome area to the east of Gyoen O-dori. Most of these bars cater to gay men, but there are a few bars for lesbians as well.

Gay bars are much smaller in Japan than in the West; discos are few. It depends, of course, on the establishment, but foreigners will find most of these places friendly and pleasant.

For details, check with the Tokyo Gay Support Group listed in the *Tokyo Journal.*

Many Japanese men are slender and sensitive by nature. Do not assume they are homosexual just by their appearance.

Love Hotels

A popular place for lovers is something called a "love hotel" (*tsurekomi hoteru* or *rabu hoteru*). The charge is calculated by the hour or by the night, and the rooms are decorated to satisfy the wildest fantasies imaginable. Of course, some are just typical hotels or traditional *ryokan,* but the rooms in even these will often come equipped with rows of mirrors or closed-circuit television. There are literally tens of thousands of these love hotels in Tokyo alone.

Turkish Baths

From 1193 to 1956 prostitution was legal, licensed, and immensely popular in Japan. When it was banned, much of it simply went underground, usually with the front of a Turkish bathhouse (*toruko*). Due to a protest from the Turkish embassy, Turkish baths now officially have a new name—"Soapland." Not all *sopurando* allow foreigners, although some cater to them, and there are a few expressly for women. The largest in the world is in Osaka. It has a total of ten floors and includes a cabaret, a garden bath, and a bath for women only.

The law requires that there be a window on each door but does not specify where. Therefore, they're usually situated in a place that offers no view—or else a towel is conveniently placed over them.

The customer is taken to a private room or "massage parlor." There he is given a bath and a massage, unless, that is, he has expressed from the outset that his real desire is to have the "special service."

23
Baths and Spas

Baths—very hot baths—are a trademark of Japan. They are part of Japanese family life, social life, and recreational life. Baths are for cleansing, soaking, relaxing—and, on occasion, talking business. Even in modern Japan, the tradition of bathing continues in the home and at hot springs and spas.

Hot Springs and Spas

One asset of Japan that most foreigners don't know to take advantage of is hot springs. Throughout Japan there are 13,300 hot springs, many of which are mineral baths with medicinal properties.

In most of these, great pains have been taken to give the impression that you are bathing outdoors in a serene natural setting (at some places you might actually be outdoors). Large windows look out to lovely landscaping, or the landscaping may be indoors—the bath having been built around massive boulders complete with grotto and ferns.

Many inns, known as *ryokan*, are located near or around these hot springs. *Ryokan* are in the traditional Japanese style—with *tatami*-mat floors, sliding doors, and meals served in the room. If you've the time and the inclination, a trip out of the city to a hot springs and *ryokan* will prove more than worth your while. The whole atmosphere of the place—rather a world unto itself—is something you won't experience anywhere else.

Bathing Etiquette

Whether you're at a hot spring or someone's home (in which case the only difference is that you'll be alone), bathing etiquette is the same. At the inn, you will probably be shown to the bath soon after arriving. This is a wonderful way to cleanse your body of the dirt and fatigue of the trip and begin your stay with a fresh spirit. At someone's home, the bath will be prepared, and you as a guest will be offered the bath first.

You will be given a small hand towel for the triple purpose of washing, drying, and protecting your modesty. When not in the bath, this is to be draped discreetly over the pubis (forget the rest of you, women, this is all that really counts). Hot springs are communal, though most these days are segregated by the sexes. Because others will be using the same water to bathe in, *soap is never to be taken into a bath.*

Upon entering the bathing room, you will find a bucket or plastic tub. With water from the bath or a faucet along the wall, dump a few bucketfuls over yourself. Although theoretically you're supposed to wash before soaking, most Japanese will get into the bath at this point. The water temperature ranges from 105 degrees to 110 degrees Fahrenheit, so get in quickly—or slowly, if that's the only way you can do it—and keep still. Moving about makes the water feel hotter.

When you do wash, you must do so outside the tub. Again, use water from the faucet or from the tub to fill your bucket with clear water; soap up your towel and wash with it. Rinse your soapy hand in this bucket of clear water and then empty the water out before dipping the bucket into the bath to refill. Use plenty of scoops of water to get off all the soap. Now you can relax in the tub once again.

Perhaps you've noticed when drying your car that a damp cloth works better than a dry one. Strangely, this applies to the human body as well. Once again, your miraculous little hand towel is there to do the job. Just make sure you wring it out well before you leave the bathing area.

If you're in a home, do *not* let the water out of the bath once you're done. The bath is to be used by the entire household.

Ryokan Etiquette

At a Japanese-style inn, you will find your room to be a basic, typically Japanese *tatami* room (or *zashiki*). There will be no furniture other than the low table in the center of the floor and probably nothing on the walls. The architecture of the room itself captures a simple natural beauty. There will be no locks on the sliding doors to your room, and you needn't concern yourself about it. You'll be surprised to find yourself feeling comfortable, secure, and private in this room. For the period of your stay, it will serve as parlor, dining room, and bedroom for you. *Do not wear shoes or slippers in it.*

Somewhere in your room you will find a light cotton kimono called a *yukata.* In most places, this is to be worn only in the confines of your room for relaxing and sleeping. At a hot-springs resort, however, you may wear it anywhere: strolling, dining, or even to a movie. Be sure that the left lapel crosses over the right; the right lapel crossing over the left symbolizes mourning. The *yukata* in your room is not to be taken with you as a souvenir. *Yukata* can usually be purchased close by.

Breakfast and dinner are usually included in your room charge. The meals will be served in your room on large lacquered trays brought up to you by the *ryokan* attendant. Most inns are aware that foreigners prefer what they're accustomed to over the Japanese breakfast of soup, fish, and rice. If that is indeed what you want, speak to the front desk and ask for *yo-shoku,* Western food. A Japanese dinner (*wa-shoku,* or Japanese food) is always to be recommended. There may be an extra fee for *yo-shoku,* and likely it won't be as good.

At night, the table will be set aside by the *ryokan* attendant, and bedding will be taken from a closet. These pads or mattresses, called *futon,* are very comfortable. The only thing you might find unaccommodating is the pillow. Rather than feathers, it's filled with buckwheat chaff and feels something like an overstuffed bean bag. There's usually a cushion in the room that you can appropriate to your purposes.

24
Incidentals

Toilets

The truly traditional Japanese toilet is a "squatter"—basically a hole over an open pit with an absolutely lethal smell. The updated version is porcelain and may or may not flush. The end to face usually has a flared protector. (A friend of mine discovered after two years in Japan that she'd been facing the wrong direction all along, when she and other members of her household were discussing why she had put a poster on the wall you didn't face!)

Toilets and baths are in separate rooms, so be sure to ask for the toilet and not a bathroom. Frequently a home will also have a urinal nestling a few naphthalene balls to combat the smell. Ladies, don't despair if you're shown to the urinal. There will be another door inside leading to the toilet stall.

Western-style toilets are gradually becoming commonplace, though many Japanese express an aversion to putting their skin on something other people have sat on. These toilets, being in an unheated part of the house, will sometimes have a heated seat or a terrycloth seat sock to take the chill off.

On many toilets you can have your choice of flushes by pushing the handle toward the 大 mark for a big flush and to the 小 for a small one.

Places that cater to foreigners will often have both a Japanese- and a Western-style toilet. In the event that you've forgotten how to use a Western one, there will often be diagrams depicting the correct method.

In many public places, there will be only one rest room for both men and women. Sometimes two separate doors—one for men and one for women—will lead into one common rest room for use by both men and women. (I can remember the first time I popped into one of these. Finding myself among a number of urinating men, I promptly exited, convinced I had my Japanese characters for men and women mixed up.) Even restaurants and bars frequently have just one room with a couple of urinals and stalls to be shared by all. It's all handled very matter-of-factly.

Hotels

Hotels in Japan are not much different from hotels everywhere except that the Japanese predilection for paying attention to detail is ever apparent.

You will often find a small refrigerator in your room stocked with a variety of beverages and snacks. Usually this works on the honor system, and it is your responsibility to record your daily consumption on the forms provided on top of the refrigerator. (At some hotels, your consumption will be registered at the front desk by way of remote control.) These forms should be brought with you when you check out. A ten-to-fifteen percent service charge is added to your bill at most hotels. This takes the place of any tipping, which is not done in Japan.

In addition to the numerous luxurious and high-priced accommodations, there are also reasonably priced business hotels (not to be confused with love hotels—see chapter 22). Capsule hotels are literally just big enough to sleep and sit in. They come with a TV and a few other amenities and of course are very inexpensive. There are reasonably priced *ryokan* (Japanese-style inns) and wildly expensive ones.

The Japan National Tourist Organization (JNTO) will send you the *Japan Hotel Guide* and *Japan Ryokan Guide* free of charge. These list prices and other helpful information. (For the JNTO office nearest you, refer to appendix C.)

Tipping

There is no tipping in Japan. It can, in fact, cause some Japanese to become indignant, as pride is taken in doing one's job well for the sheer service of it. (An elderly professor told me that when he first came to the United States in his youth, his first job was as a delivery boy for a pharmacy. After making his first delivery in the hilly terrain of San Francisco, the kindly customer called after him and tossed him a dime. The young man caught the dime, but then, realizing it was money, threw it back at the customer. This was the young man's last delivery.)

If you feel particularly grateful to a maid or someone else, a small gift would be appropriate—or just a sincere expression of thanks, especially in Japanese. A service charge is usually added to hotel and some restaurant bills, but in any case, no further gratuity is either expected or wanted.

Traditionally "tea money" (*chadai*) was given to the proprietors on one's arrival at or departure from an inn. This money, shared among the servants, would of course be in a proper envelope or at least wrapped in white paper.

Electricity

Japan uses 100 volts, A.C., although many hotels have 110- and 220-volt outlets to accommodate Western appliances. Electricity is 50 cycles in the eastern part (Tokyo) and 60 cycles in the western part (Osaka, Kyoto, and Nagoya). Appliances made for 60 cycles will run more slowly in Tokyo; those set for 50 cycles will run more quickly (and therefore get hotter) in Osaka. This means you could damage or burn out the motor in your appliance unless there is "50/60 hertz" written on it.

Banks

Bank hours are 9:00 A.M. to 3:00 P.M. Monday through Friday, 9:00 A.M. to noon on Saturdays (but banks are closed on the second Saturday of each month). If you wish to convert more than seventy-two thousand yen into foreign currency, you must apply for a license at the foreign currency section of a major bank. Bring your passport, residence certificate, and airline ticket.

Checks and Credit Cards

Personal checks are not accepted anywhere. However, traveler's checks are taken at major banks, hotels, some *ryokan,* and large stores in the larger cities. International credit cards are also accepted at major establishments.

Shopping

Typical quality souvenirs from Japan include pearls, silks, watches, radios, cameras, cloisonné, lacquerware, pottery, woodblock prints, chinaware, dolls, fans, and paper lanterns.

Small shops off the beaten track tend to have more flavor, but many of the items mentioned above may be purchased tax-free at designated stores. You will find tax-free shops in airports, near or in your hotel, and in some of the large underground shopping malls. You will need to present your passport and keep the documentation they give you.

Department stores usually close around six o'clock in the evening and are often closed on one weekday. Haggling is not done in these or other fixed-price stores, though bargaining is sometimes done in a subtle fashion in art, antique, and tourist shops.

For electronic items, the area of Akihabara in Tokyo is the place to go. There are literally thousands of large, tiny, and very competitive shops. Look for tax-free signs. One can bargain at stores in Akihabara.

The Ginza is a very colorful and lively district full of large and small stores alike, selling all kinds of merchandise. Note that barber shops are closed on Tuesdays and gas stations on Sundays.

Available free of charge from the Japan National Tourist Organization is a directory of stores, listed by the merchandise they carry, called *Souvenirs of Japan.*

Immigration

Americans and Australians need visas. Citizens of New Zealand do not need visas for stays up to thirty days; citizens of Canada, France, Denmark, Spain, and most of South America can stay without a visa for up to ninety days; and citizens of the United Kingdom, Mexico, Switzerland, Germany, and Austria can stay without a visa for up to one hundred eighty days. See appendix E for types of visas.

If you plan to stay longer than ninety days at one time, you must apply for alien registration at your city or ward office. Bring your passport and three five-by-five-centimeter photographs. Passports must be carried with you at all times until you obtain an alien registration; then the registration card must be carried.

When dealing with immigration, expect it to take time. Go early, when the crowds are small. If you work for a prominent Japanese company and fear you will have problems, a phone call ahead of time from the right person can make a difference.

Refer to appendix E for addresses of immigration offices throughout Japan.

Controlled Substances

Narcotics are highly controlled substances, carrying severe fines and jail sentences. Marijuana is not at all socially accepted. It would be wise to confine your indulgences to alcohol during your stay in Japan.

25
Living in Japan

If you are going to Japan to live, the first thing to deal with when taking up residence is culture shock. Your ability to deal with this will determine how much enjoyment you will get out of your first six months—the critical months.

Adjusting to any foreign culture is not easy, but adapting to one as alien as Japan can be a problem. One recommendation of psychologists is to make friends, both Japanese and foreign, as soon as possible. Your Japanese friends will help you understand why things are done the way they are. Your foreign friends will help you to see how the adjustment is made and offer you a release for pent-up reactions. If you work, take time to socialize with your fellow workers after hours. If you don't work, it's possible to meet people by taking up a traditional art form or some other cultural study.

Another piece of advice is to get out of your environment once a month. This means taking a day or two to go someplace out in the country, perhaps a hot spring, or at least to another town.

Avoid the urge to get angry and frustrated when things are slow or seem absurd. It's good to take stock regularly why you are there. It is certainly not wise to complain or to be critical. Remember that things will seem confusing when cultural and language barriers exist. When this happens, it's easy to assume that the behavior of others is irregular.

There are centers which provide workshops on adaptation

skills. Advertisements for these can sometimes be seen in the *Tokyo Journal.*

See appendix B for some useful telephone numbers to help you through the more difficult times.

Housing

Finding living quarters anywhere in Japan is not an easy task, but least of all in Tokyo. Rents are high, especially if you want to avoid a long (and usually horrendous) morning commute.

In your search for a place to live, you will probably come across the term "mansion" (*manshon*). These are simply more deluxe and expensive quarters than the tiny rooms they call "apartments" (*apaato*).

Your best method of search will probably be through ads in English-language newspapers and through your acquaintances. Foreigners frequently turn their apartments over to other foreigners when they leave. Any Japanese acquaintance might know someone who knows someone who could give you an important introduction.

Don't be offended if a landlord refuses to rent to you. Foreigners are short-term tenants who usually don't know the customs or the language.

Be prepared to pay a handsome deposit fee. This *shikikin,* or *hoshokin,* is returned to you when you leave. However, *kenrikin,* "key money" (sometimes called *reikin,* "thank-you money"), is *not* refundable. The general rule is that to move into an apartment or house in Tokyo, be prepared to put out about five times your monthly rent (two months' rent for *shikikin,* one month's rent for *reikin,* another month's rent to the agent, plus the first month's rent). Only a portion of this will be returned when you leave.

When paying rent (or lesson fees or anything else of that nature), be sure to put the money in an envelope. Your landlord (or teacher) may provide you with one to be reused each month. If he or she does not, you may purchase one for this specific purpose. In the event that you don't have one, any envelope will do.

Visiting

In addition to the New Year's and mid-year festivities, there are a few other occasions when calls should be made. These are for such purposes as inquiring after an accident or illness (*o-mimai*), for offering congratulations on auspicious occasions, and when one moves into a new neighborhood. In this last instance, the new person should visit his neighbors on both sides and the three across the street. Buckwheat noodles, being long and thin, were traditionally given to new neighbors, symbolizing the desire for the acquaintanceship to be long, even if it is "thin." (This is also a pun, as *soba* means both "noodles" and "in the vicinity.") If one is the recipient of any of the above visits, return visits should be paid to express thanks with "*Senjitsu wa domo arigato gozaimashita.*"

At the above times, you should expect just to stand in the entranceway, because once a guest enters the house, it becomes a social call. If you are invited in, however, you should not stay more than thirty minutes. At this time you should say, "*Taihen nagaku o jama itashimashita. Kore de shitsurei sasete itadakimasu,*" or "Please excuse me now, I have bothered you for a long time."

Your host or hostess may, out of politeness, insist that you stay longer. You should refuse this with "*Arigato gozaimasu ga, shitsurei sasete itadakimasu*" ("Thank you very much, but I humbly beg you to let me commit this rudeness"). You should insist that they not see you to the door (*dozo, o-kamai naku*), though they will insist on doing so. Bow as you leave the room and again in the *genkan* as you say thanks. Then excuse yourself before you go out the door with "*shitsurei shimasu*" ("Excuse this my rudeness").

Japanese are known to say as Westerners might "Stop by whenever you're in the area," or "We're always home on Sundays—stop by anytime." In most cases, these are just polite words and are not to be taken seriously. On the other hand, sometimes you'll find that they will stop in because they were in the neighborhood. If someone visits without calling first, you are under less obligation to entertain and feed them properly.

Foreign Wives in Japan

If you are a Western woman living in or visiting Japan with your husband (or boyfriend), it will be easier on you if you are aware of the cultural differences that affect you. If your husband is working with the Japanese, your understanding and acceptance of the customs in Japan will greatly contribute to your husband's success and your own ease.

The main area in which you will feel the difference is entertainment. Your husband will be requested and expected to "go out with the boys" frequently, and it will be necessary that he do so to establish close relationships. Even if invitations are extended to you, it would be better if he made an excuse for you; the Japanese will be more comfortable if it's just the men.

If you are living in Japan, establish your own circle of friends or get to know the wives of your husband's colleagues. If you invite your husband's Japanese associate and his wife to your home, don't be surprised if the wife doesn't come. If she does, it would be Japanese-like of you to invite her to join you in the kitchen and spend your own time there when not serving.

If you are just visiting Japan with your husband, sign up for tours and other things to occupy your time. Maybe one of the Japanese wives or female office workers can accompany you shopping. Understand that the demands put on your husband will be different than in the West. Be prepared for the custom of "men first."

Coming Prepared

The only way to soften the blow of adapting to an alien culture is to prepare yourself as much as possible. Along with language training, try to get as much education on the customs as you can. Take advantage of the many good books available (see appendix F).

Familiarizing yourself with the food ahead of time is not a major problem these days. Most Western cities have an ample variety of Japanese restaurants (although be wary of obvious deviations such as mayonnaise on *sushi*), and it would be wise to acquaint yourself with them.

When times do get hard, don't forget to look to others for help. Every other expatriate before you has had to go through the adjustment and can relate, in varying degrees, to what you're experiencing. Then, too, don't forget to prepare yourself for the culture shock of returning home, which may be much worse.

VII

GENERAL INFORMATION

26
Facts on Japan

Geography

Japan is made up of four large islands and about four thousand small islands, with an aggregate size slightly smaller than California. The largest of the islands is Honshu, containing the capital, Tokyo, and the major cities Yokohama, Osaka, Nagoya, and Kyoto. Honshu is followed in size by Hokkaido, the northernmost island, Kyushu, the southernmost, and Shikoku, the smallest. Four-fifths of Japan is unarable, mountainous land.

Population

The current population of Japan is 117 million. The populations of major cities, as of March 1984, are as follows:

Tokyo	8,170,000
Yokohama	2,915,000
Osaka	2,534,000
Nagoya	2,066,000
Sapporo	1,479,000
Kyoto	1,464,000
Kobe	1,381,000
Fukuoka	1,098,000
Kitakyushu	1,052,000
Kawasaki	1,049,000

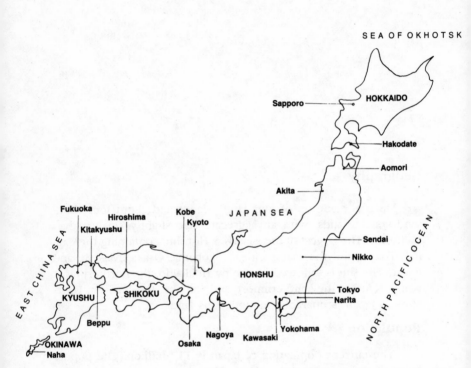

Climate

Tokyo temperatures range from thirty-two to fifty degrees
Fahrenheit (zero to ten degrees Celsius) in the winter and eighty-
six to ninety-five degrees Fahrenheit (thirty to thirty-five degrees

Celsius) in the summer. The southern islands tend to be warmer all year around. Kyoto and Osaka are colder than Tokyo in the winter and more hot and humid in summer. The rainy season throughout Japan is mid-June to mid-July. Tokyo gets snow a couple of times a year. Northern Honshu and Hokkaido generally have snow October through March.

Religion

Although the Japanese are not often thought by Westerners to be religious, in many ways the religion of Japan is inseparable from the fabric of Japanese life itself. It is a mixture of Shintoism, Buddhism, and Confucianism. The three have been made to fit compatibly together, and each is thought to play its own role in various aspects of Japanese life. None of these involves going regularly to a place of worship, but many families have both Buddhist and Shinto altars at which respect is paid regularly.

Shintoism is the name given to the indigenous native worship of Japan to distinguish it from Buddhism. In the past, all living things, inanimate objects, and natural phenomena were thought to have a spiritual essence that was revered. Harmony and the inseparability of man and nature were a strong part of Shinto beliefs.

Every clan had its own guardian deity, usually thought to have been an ancestor. The clan from which the emperor is descended worshipped the sun goddess, and as the power of this clan increased, so did the importance of the sun goddess.

The places of Shinto worship are called shrines (*jinja*) and can be distinguished by the red wooden archways before them.

Buddhism was brought to Japan in the sixth century A.D. from Korea. It teaches nonviolence and respect for all living things (*geta*, the Japanese wooden—as opposed to leather shoes—were a result of the Buddhist ban on killing animals). Shinto concerns itself with life and living things, while Buddhism addresses death and the afterlife. Funerals are still overwhelmingly Buddhist affairs.

Zen, which literally translates into "silent meditation," was brought from China around the thirteenth century. Zen concentrates on discipline and austerity, teaching one to look for the Buddha within and to live this fleeting life with dignity and calm.

Buddhist places of worship are called temples, *tera,* and usually have names that end in *ji* (another reading of the character for "temple").

More a philosophy than a religion, Confucianism places strong importance on duty, filial piety, and loyalty to superiors. The five basic relationships that must be properly maintained are lord/subject, father/son, husband/wife, older brother/younger brother, and friend/friend.

This emphasis on the proper relationship between lord/subject was greatly taken advantage of by the Tokugawa rulers in the seventeenth and eighteenth centuries. It is primarily responsible for the vertical social system that exists in Japan today.

Christianity began in Japan with the arrival of Francis Xavier and two other Jesuit missionaries in 1549. For a variety of reasons, Catholicism was well received and spread from their port of landing in Kyushu through southern Japan. By the early 1600s, Catholics claimed over 200,000 converts.

Struggle for political power between Christian sects led to the banishment of foreign missionaries and to persecution of converts. Many Christians died and many reverted to indigenous religions, but at least four thousand Christians and their descendants went underground for 225 years until a Roman Catholic church was constructed in Nagasaki in 1865.

Today there are about 930,000 Christians in Japan, or under one percent of the population. There are a number of Christian universities, of which the best known are Sophia and the International Christian University in Tokyo, and Doshisha in Kyoto. (To locate a Christian or Jewish place of worship, see appendix B.)

27
Transportation and Telephone Hints

Air Travel

There are three major domestic Japanese airlines: Japan Air Lines, All Nippon Airways, and Toa Domestic Airlines. You may purchase tickets at a travel agency or at an airport. JAL has tickets available in vending machines for the Tokyo–Osaka flights.

Reservations may be made by calling the airlines directly as well as through an agency. International return flights should be reconfirmed seventy-two hours before departure.

A two-thousand-yen passenger service facility charge will be required at check-in for all adults leaving from Narita Airport, Tokyo.

Railways

The *shinkansen,* popularly referred to as the bullet train, has the reputation of being the fastest and most punctual in the world. It's a well-earned reputation. A train leaves Tokyo every fifteen minutes.

The *shinkansen* will take you from Tokyo to Kyoto in three hours, from Tokyo to Kobe in three and a half hours, and from Tokyo to Beppu in eight and a half, including a change in trains. Going north from Tokyo, it is four hours to Sendai and seventeen hours to Sapporo.

Reserved seats and express trains (such as the *shinkansen*) cost extra. First class is called the Green Car. Tickets may be purchased at special windows displaying a green clover leaf.

The bullet train has a dining car as well as a stand-up buffet car for coffee, drinks, and snacks. Vendors also come through the aisles regularly selling box lunches (*bento*), coffee, tangerines, and snacks.

If you are flying JAL, JAL will make *shinkansen* arrangements for you from the United States or Canada. Otherwise, you will have to make reservations through an authorized travel agent.

Shinkansen tickets can be purchased at almost any large station in Tokyo. Travel Service Centers, called *Ryoko Centa* which has someone who speaks English, are open from 9:00 A.M. to 6:00 P.M. Monday through Friday. You can find them also at many of the large stations.

For a view of Mount Fuji on your way west, sit on the right side of the train (C or D seat). Mount Fuji will come into view about forty-five minutes out of Tokyo.

Japan Rail Passes for seven, fourteen, and twenty-one days are available through travel agents, but these passes *must* be purchased *outside* Japan.

Information on fares and timetables for all of Japanese public transportation can be obtained from the Japan National Tourist Organization, Japan Travel Bureau Offices, and Tourist Information Centers. (See appendix C for locations.)

When traveling during the long holidays (New Year's, May, July, and, in some areas, August), be sure to reserve well in advance. Note that all cars are smoking cars. If you want a nonsmoking car, you'll have to sit in the last car, which has no reserved seats, from Tokyo to Osaka, or the first car from Osaka to Tokyo.

The *shinkansen* is not equipped to handle much luggage. Up to two pieces may be carried on and stored in the overhead racks. Three additional pieces weighing up to 198 pounds (90 kilograms) may be checked.

Stops are very brief, so be ready to exit with all your luggage as soon as the train stops.

Porters can be found only at major stations; they charge a set fee.

Taxis

When taking a taxi from an airport or a train station, you will find two lines for two sizes of taxis and, of course, two prices. The larger and more expensive taxis usually have the shorter line. Queue up in front of the sign of the taxi size you want. When your turn arrives, don't attempt to open the car door yourself. The driver will do this for you by means of a lever by his seat. Warning: standing back saves shins.

Many taxis have miniature television sets in them for your enjoyment.

Wherever you're taking a taxi, if your destination is other than a popularly known or public place, it is *imperative* that you have directions written in detail, in Japanese, on a piece of paper that you can hand to the driver. It is virtually impossible to find a residence by mere address. Not only are buildings not numbered consecutively, but dozens of places may have the same address. Always carry a card or matchbook from your hotel.

Every mile or so there will be a small police booth with a couple of policemen who can help point you where you want to go.

Taxis are reasonable, but there is a substantial additional fee for the hours between 11:00 P.M. and 5:00 A.M. Getting a taxi between 11:00 and 11:30 P.M. can be extremely difficult, as this is when the nightclubs close. Do not expect the driver to have change for anything over a thousand-yen bill.

Avoid rush hours on all surface transportation: 7:30–9:00 A.M., 5:00–6:30 P.M. Allow much more time to travel across Tokyo by taxi at any time than you would in most other cities in the world.

Telephones

You can call anywhere in Japan on any public phone. The phones come in different colors and have different capacities:
Red phones take ten-yen coins up to six at a time.
Blue phones take ten-yen coins up to ten at a time.

Yellow phones take ten-yen coins up to ten or hundred-yen coins up to nine.

Green phones take ten-yen and hundred-yen coins and credit cards.

A dial tone will be audible only after inserting a coin. Ten yen will buy a three-minute local call or a shorter long-distance call. A faint warning sound means you are out of time and must quickly insert another coin (or coins for long distance). To be sure you don't get cut off, add plenty of coins; the warning tone is hard to hear. Any coins not required by your call will be returned to you.

Travel and other information is available in English from blue, yellow, or private phones. (Refer to appendix B for this and other useful numbers.)

28
Holidays and Festivals

This chapter is provided to help you take advantage of some of Japan's rich traditions, and also to help you to avoid times when businesses might be closed or travel difficult.

The two times to avoid are Golden Week (April 29 through May 5) and *o-bon* week. During Golden Week, the Japanese flock to every tourist spot in the country, and every form of transportation is packed. *O-bon* is tricky because in some areas it's mid-July and in others it's mid-August, but it's the time when people return to their hometowns to honor their ancestors. New Year's, as in the West, is a time when people are inaccessible.

National Holidays

(When a holiday falls on a Sunday, it is observed on a Monday.)

January 1 through 3: New Year's celebrations
  (some places close until the 6th)
January 15: Adults' Day
February 11: National Foundation Day
March 20 or 21: Vernal Equinox Day
April 29: Emperor's Birthday
May 3: Constitution Memorial Day
May 5: Children's Day
September 15: Respect for the Aged Day

September 23 or 24: Autumnal Equinox Day
October 10: Health-Sports Day
November 3: Culture Day
November 23: Labor Thanksgiving Day

Festivals and Celebrations

The Japanese love festivals, and a festival can be observed any day of the year somewhere in the country. The following traditional holidays are observed nationwide and with an enthusiasm seen only at Christmastime in the West:

January 1 through 3: *O-shogatsu.* This is a time for dressing in one's best kimono. People visit temples, shrines, friends, and relatives, greeting all with, *"Shinnen akemashete, o-medeto gozaimasu."* An informal New Year's meeting is held on the first day back at work. Great effort is made to start the new year on a positive note.

February 3 or 4: *Setsubun,* the bean-throwing ceremony. At homes, shrines, and temples, people fervently throw beans at invisible "devils" and recite, "Out with the devil, in with good fortune!"

March 3: Girls' Day. Elaborate and very expensive sets of dolls are displayed in homes and public places.

March 20 or 21: *Higan.* The Vernal Equinox is a time when people visit ancestral graves. It celebrates the coming of spring.

April 29: The Emperor's birthday is the start of Golden Week.

May 1: May Day is a time for peaceful protests by Socialists, Communists, and labor unions.

May 5: Children's Day used to be Boys' Day. Carp-shaped streamers are hung from bamboo poles. (Carps symbolize strength.)

July 7: *Tanabata* Star Festival. This honors the time when the Weaver Girl on one side of the Milky Way is permitted to meet with her lover, the Shepherd Boy, on the other side. Poems and wishes are written on colored slips of paper and tied to bamboo.

July 15 or August 15: *O-bon.* The celebration in honor of dead ancestors. The exact date depends on the moon and the locality. People return to their hometowns and set out lanterns to light the way back for their ancestors. Bonfires in the shape of certain characters are lit on the hills around Kyoto. Presents called *o-chugen* are given.

September 23: Autumnal Equinox. Again, a time to honor one's ancestors.

October 10: Sports Day commemorates the 1964 Olympics in Tokyo.

November 3: Culture Day, previously the Meiji Emperor's birthday.

November 15: Seven-Five-Three festival. For girls aged seven and three, and boys of five and three. Parents dress the children in new and expensive attire, then take them to shrines and thank the gods for their survival through the early years.

December: *Bonenkai* parties are held in offices and with one's friends to "forget the old year." Christmas celebrations are often incorporated into it. Presents called *o-seibo* are given.

December 31: New Year's Eve is to be spent with the family. At midnight, temples ring their bells 108 times to cleanse people of the 108 sins man is supposed to be guilty of.

APPENDICES

Appendix A
Printers of Japanese Business Cards

Having your business cards printed in Japanese is one indication of your interest and commitment in doing business with the Japanese. In addition to the following list of printers, many airlines provide this service for their customers. Also, some of the major hotels in Japan provide, for a fee, overnight card printing. For a more professional job, though, contact one of the following printers in your area.

To make sure you are able to present your cards with the Japanese right side up, have the Japanese printed horizontally with the top of the Japanese side of the card being the same as the English version on the reverse side.

United States

Los Angeles:

Japan Graphics
202 South San Pedro St.
Los Angeles, CA 90012
(213) 687-3454

Zero Graphics
424 Boyd St.
Los Angeles, CA 90013
(213) 680-0253

San Francisco:

KK Graphic Printing
1485 Bayshore Blvd.
San Francisco, CA 94108
(415) 468-1057

China Cultural Printing Co.
918 Clay St.
San Francisco, CA 94108
(415) 956-1240

Seattle:

Japan Pacific Publications
P.O. Box 3092
Seattle, WA 98114
(206) 622-7443

West Coast Printing, Inc.
622 Rainier Avenue S.
Seattle, WA 98144
(206) 323-0441

Chicago:

Japanese Arts & Communications
P.O. Box 11203
612 N. Michigan Ave.
Chicago, IL 60611
(312) 664-3984

New York:

Hikari Japanese Typesetting
481 8th Ave.
New York, NY 10001
(212) 947-1659

Japan Printing Services
17 John St.
New York, NY 10038
(212) 406-2905

Nihon Services Corp.
1 Union Square West, Rm. 208
New York, NY 10003
(212) 929-6022

Japan Typesetting and Graphics
342 Madison Ave.
New York, NY 10173
(212) 687-0086

Australia

Nichigo Press
6/12 Cross St.
Double Bay NSW 2028
02-327-2908

Miyako Print
329 Little Collins St.
Melbourne, VIC 3000
03-63-5500

Canada

Bluetree Graphics
503-353 Water St.
Vancouver, B.C. V6B 1B8
(604) 688-0303

Japan Graphics
669 Denman St.
Vancouver, B.C. V6G 2L3
(604) 688-7636

France

Edition Ilyfunet
57, rue Jules Ferry
94120 Fontenay-sous-Bois

Intra Service
(Tozai Doryu Center)
Gerant: M. Tingaud
82, rue de la Victoire
75009 Paris

West Germany

Dai Nippon Printing GmbH
Steinstr. 30
40000 Dusseldorf 1
0211-320206

Kern-Druckerei
Larchenstr. 7
6368 Bad Vibel 4
(near Frankfurt)
06101-6746

Great Britain

Stephen Austin and Sons, Ltd.
Caxton Hill
Hertford SG137LU
0992-54955

IPMC Translation
25 Marloes Road
London W8 6LG
01-373-0464

JTS-Japanese Translation Services
9 Serpentine Rd.
Selly Park
Birmingham B29 7HU
021-472-7703

Mantra (London), Ltd.
4 West End Ave., Pinner
Middlesen HA5 1BJ
01-866-9438

Mitaka
188-189 Drury Lane
London WC2R 5QD
01-405-2202

Netherlands

Drukkerij E.J. Brill
Plantynstraat 2
P.O. Box 9000
2300 Pa Leiden
071-146646

New Zealand

Fuji Enterprises
P.O. Box 4558
Auckland
773-302

Japan/New Zealand Publications,
Ltd.
P.O. Box 36-166
Auckland
798-196

Appendix B
Survival Numbers

Emergencies

Police	110
Fire	119
Ambulance	119

General Information

Directory assistance	104
Directory assistance outside the area code	105
International telephoning information	
in Tokyo	270-5111
in Osaka	228-2300

Note that the phone numbers listed below are for Tokyo, unless otherwise indicated. For numbers not listed here, consult the Yellow Pages in the English Telephone Directory available in bookstores or at your hotel.

The Tokyo area code is 03. When calling from Tokyo, it is unnecessary to use this prefix.

Bullet train	
to call a passenger	248-9311
Travel information (in English)	
in Tokyo	502-1461
in Kyoto	371-5649
when calling outside of these areas for information regarding:	
Eastern Japan	0120-222-800
Western Japan	0120-444-800
Teletourist taped message	
in English	503-2911
in French	503-2926
in Kyoto	361-2911
Japan Guide Association	213-2766
American Pharmacy	271-4034

Lost and found
Tokyo Metropolitan Police	814-4151
Japan National Railway (JNR)	
at Tokyo Station	231-1880
at Ueno Station	841-8061
Subways	834-5577
Buses	216-2953
Taxis	355-0300

(If not recovered in three to five days, items are usually taken to the metropolitan police.)

Counseling and Referrals

Alcoholics Anonymous	431-8357
Association of Foreign Wives	
(see notices in English-language newspapers)	
International Social Services	711-5551
Tokyo Community Counseling	
Services	398-4390
Tokyo English Lifeline	264-4347

Judeo-Christian Places of Worship

Tokyo
Baha'i Faith	209-7521
Franciscan Chapel Center	401-2141
Jewish Community Center	400-2559
Religious Society of Friends	451-7002
Saint Alban's Church	431-8534
Saint Ignatius Church	263-4584
Tokyo Baptist Church	461-8425
Tokyo International Church	464-4512
Tokyo Union Church	400-0047
Tokyo Unitarian Church	409-8051

Osaka
Cathedral Church	581-5061
Osaka International Church	768-4385

Appendix C
Helpful Organizations

The JAPAN EXTERNAL TRADE ORGANIZATION (JETRO), known outside of Japan as the JAPAN TRADE CENTER, is a nonprofit organization set up to promote foreign trade and commerce in Japan. The organization maintains extensive listings of Japanese companies—by commodity—and has available free brochures on just about every aspect of business in Japan. It will set up seminars and offer consultation and evaluation of proposed projects. It also publishes a ten-page newsletter with reports and analyses of Japan's economy, policies, and market opportunities.

United States—Japan Trade Council, Inc.
100 Connecticut Avenue, N.W.
Washington, D.C. 20036
202-296-5633

Japan Trade Center
(in the United States)
  McGraw-Hill Building
  1221 Avenue of the Americas
  Forty-fourth Floor
  New York, NY 10020-1060
  212-997-0400

  230 North Michigan Avenue
  Chicago, IL 60601
  312-726-4390

One Houston Center
1221 McKenney Street
Suite 1810
Houston, TX 77010
713-759-9595

555 South Flower Street
Los Angeles, CA 90071
213-626-5700

Qantas Building
360 Post Street
Suite 501
San Francisco, CA 94108
415-392-1333

Japan Trade Center (in Canada)
  Britannica House
  151 Bloor Street West
  Suite 700
  Toronto, Ontario M5S IT7
  416-962-5050

Royal Bank Building
10117 Jasper Avenue
Room 812
Edmonton, Alberta T5J 1W8
403-428-0866

Place Bonaventure
50 Frontenac
Floor F
Montreal, Quebec 114 PQ
514-861-5240

Standard Building
510 West Hastings Street
Room 916
Vancouver, British Columbia
 V6B 1L8
604-684-4174

Japan Trade Center
Martini Building
50 Avenue Deschamps-Elysees
Paris 8, France
225-3582

Japan Trade Center
19/25 Baker Street
London W1M 1AE England
486-6761

Japan Trade Center
Colonnaden 72
2000 Hamburg 36
Bundesrepublik Deutschland
West Germany
341-7635

Japan External Trade Organization
 (JETRO)
 2-5 Toranomon, 2-chome
 Minato-ku, Tokyo 105
 03-582-5511

 Over-the-Counter Service
 International Information
  Service
 JETRO

 International Lounge
 International Communication
  Department
 JETRO

Bingomachi Building
Suite 2051
Higashi-ku, Osaka 541
06-203-3601

Aichi Trade Center
4-7 Marunouchi, 2-chome
Naka-ku, Nagoya 460
052-211-4517

The MANUFACTURED IMPORTS PROMOTION ORGANIZATION (MIPRO) makes available to interested parties information and catalogs of Western manufacturers with operations in Japan. It also sponsors trade fairs and holds, in Japan, exhibitions that feature foreign commodities.

Manufactured Imports Promotion Organization
Japanese Division
2000 L Street, N.W.
Suite 808
Washington, D.C. 20036
202-659-3729

The EXPORT-IMPORT BANK OF JAPAN is a wholly governmentally owned financial institution working to promote foreign exports to and imports from Japan. It will lend money for joint Japanese-foreign trade ventures.

Export-Import Bank of Japan
1707 8th Street, N.W.
Suite 801
Washington, D.C. 20006
202-331-8547

Export-Import Bank of Japan
1-4-1 Otemachi
Chiyoda-ku, Tokyo 100
03-287-1221

Export-Import Bank of Japan
Nissei Midosuji Building
Tenth Floor
2-4 Minami-senba, 4-chome
Minami-ku, Osaka 542
06-241-1771

The JAPAN DEVELOPMENT BANK is a noncommercial, governmentally owned financial institution that will extend loans to Japanese and foreign-affiliated corporations *in Japan.* Loans are for establishing fixed assets, such as factories, and *not* for operations. There is a special loan program for furthering international industrial cooperation in Japan.

Japan Development Bank
71 Broadway
New York, NY 10006
212-297-0527

Japan Development Bank
1019 19th Street, N.W.
Suite 600
Washington, D.C. 20036
202-331-8696

Japan Development Bank
9-1 Otemachi, 1-chome
Chiyoda-ku, Tokyo 100
03-270-3211
International Department:
03-245-0439

The U.S. DEPARTMENT OF COMMERCE can supply interested parties with details on trade fairs. Persons planning to export to Japan can make use of the Department's agency-distributor service to help find an agent.

U.S. Department of Commerce
14th Street and Constitution Avenue, N.W.
Washington, D.C. 20230
202-377-2867

The U.S. INTERNATIONAL TRADE COMMISSION has compiled international trade studies, uniform statistical data, and tariff schedules of the United States.

U.S. International Trade Commission
701 E Street, N.W.
Washington, D.C. 20436
202-523-0235

In Japan, the BUSINESS INFORMATION CENTER or COMMERCIAL BRANCH of the EMBASSY OF THE UNITED STATES OF AMERICA can help establish contacts, provide assistance for conducting business in Japan, and even help negotiate with government officials. At the Center's vast library can be found a wealth of information on Japanese companies. The Center also publishes the *Japan Market Information Report.*

Embassy of the United States of America
10-5 Akasaka, 1-chome
Minato-ku, Tokyo 107
03-583-7141
Business Information Center: extension 681

The FEDERATION OF ECONOMIC ORGANIZATIONS, or *Keidanren,* is Japan's most powerful business organization. It is industry's spokesperson to the Japanese government. It does copious amounts of research on economic issues and will act as a go-between for its various constituent firms.

Federation of Economic Organizations
Keidanren Kaikan
9-4 Otemachi, 1-chome
Chiyoda-ku, Tokyo 100
03-279-1411

The JAPAN INSTITUTE FOR SOCIAL AND ECONOMIC AFFAIRS, or *Keizai Koho Center,* is a nonprofit organization that works cooperatively with the above Federation of Economic Organizations.

Japan Institute for Social and Economic Affairs
Keizai Koho Center
6-1 Otemachi, 1-chome
Chiyoda-ku, Tokyo 100
03-201-1415

Important governmental resources in Japan include the following:

Ministry of International Trade and Industry (MITI)
Information Office
1-3-1 Kasumigaseki
Chiyoda-ku, Tokyo 100
03-501-1511

Ministry of Foreign Affairs
Public Information and Cultural Affairs Bureau
2-1-2 Kasumigaseki
Chiyoda-ku, Tokyo 100
03-580-3311

The AMERICAN CHAMBER OF COMMERCE OF JAPAN can be one of the most useful organizations to join for persons planning to establish operations in Japan. The Chamber researches various critical aspects of commerce in Japan for American businesses: patents and trademarks, employment practices, taxation, financial services, small-business expansion, investments, and trade expansion. Members of the Chamber receive its monthly *Journal* in addition to a newsletter, books, and manuals. The Chamber also sponsors programs and seminars of current interest.

American Chamber of Commerce of Japan (ACCJ)
Fukide Building #2
Seventh Floor
1-21 Toranomon, 4-chome
Minato-ku, Tokyo 105
03-433-5381

JAPANESE BANKS are a good source of information as well as contacts with wholesalers and retailers. They have available information regarding competition, new technology, interested parties and their credit ratings, the Japanese marketplace, and legal issues.

GENERAL TRADING COMPANIES, or *sogo-shosha*, besides facilitating the flow of imports and exports throughout the world, are involved in commerce at many other levels. They can provide information such as market conditions as well as supply contacts, distribution channels, and access to their great intelligence-gathering arm. They act as *shokai-sha, chukai-sha*, freight forwarders, financiers, coordinators, and organizers, and they are frequently involved in joint ventures.

If one is dealing with a relatively small volume, SPECIALIZED TRADING COMPANIES, or *shosha*, might be the better way to go. The companies can provide a more personalized service than the enormous general trading companies.

Many of the MAJOR HOTELS in Japan have BUSINESS INFORMATION SERVICE CENTERS that may be particularly helpful for foreign businessmen. Here, one can arrange for interpreters, secretarial assistance, and equipment rental.

The JAPAN NATIONAL TOURIST ORGANIZATION (JNTO), a governmental organization created to promote tourism to Japan, has available at offices around the world, as well as in Japan, brochures, books, films, and general materials on Japan.

JNTO United States
   45 Rockefeller Plaza
   New York, NY 10020

   333 North Michigan Avenue
   Chicago, IL 60601

   2270 Kalakaua Avenue
   Honolulu, HI 96815

   1420 Commerce Street
   Dallas, TX 75201

   624 Grand Avenue
   Los Angeles, CA 90017

   1737 Post Street
   San Francisco, CA 94115

JNTO Australia
115 Pitt Street
Sydney, N.S.W. 2000

JNTO Canada
165 University Avenue
Toronto, Ontario M5H 3B8

JNTO England
167 Regent Street
London W1

JNTO France
4-8 Rue Sainte-Anne
75001 Paris

JNTO Mexico
Reforma 122
5th Floor, B-2
Mexico 6, D.F.

JNTO Switzerland
Rue de Berne 13
Geneva

JNTO West Germany
Biebergasse 6-10
6000 Frankfurt a/M

The JAPAN TRAVEL BUREAU (JTB) is Japan's largest travel agency. In addition to travel assistance throughout Japan, it will provide resource material on Japanese culture and history as produced by the Bureau's huge publishing division.

Other important resources include the following:

Embassy of the United States
10-5 Akasaka, 1-chome
Minato-ku, Tokyo 107
03-583-7141

Consulates of the United States
   Sankei Building
   27 Umeda-cho
   Kita-ku, Osaka
   06-341-2754

5-26 Ohori, 2-chome
Chuo-ku, Fukuoka
092-751-9331

10 Kano-cho, 6-chome
Ikuta-ku, Kobe
978-331-9679

1 Nishi, 13-chome, Kita 1-jo
Chuo-ku, Sapporo
011-221-5121

2129 Gusukuma
Urasoe, Naha, Okinawa
0988-77-8142

American Center Library
ABC Building
20603 Siba Koen
Minato-ku, Tokyo
03-436-0901

1-3-36 Tenjin
Chuo-ku, Fukuoka
092-761-6667

657 Higashi Monzen-cho
Sokokuji
Kamigyo-ku, Kyoto
075-241-1211

Yokota Building
2028-24 Izumi
Higashi-ku, Nagoya
052-931-8907

Sankei Building
27 Umeda-cho
Kita-ku, Osaka
06-345-0601

Nishi 12, Kita 2
Chuo-ku, Sapporo
011-251-9211

Embassy of Canada
3-38 Akasaka, 7-chome
Minato-ku, Tokyo 105
03-408-2101

Embassy of France
11-44 Azabu, 4-chome
Minato-ku, Tokyo 106
03-473-0171

Embassy of Great Britain
1 Ichiban-cho
Chiyoda-ku, Tokyo 102
03-265-5511

Embassy of West Germany
5-10 Minami-azabu, 4-chome
Minato-ku, Tokyo 106
03-473-0151

Embassy of Japan
(in the United States)
2520 Massachusetts Avenue, N.W.
Washington, D.C. 20008-2869
202-234-2266

Consulates of Japan
(in the United States)
    909 West Ninth Avenue
    Suite 301
    Anchorage, AK 99501
    907-279-8428

400 Colony Square Building
Suite 1501
1201 Peachtree Street, N.E.
Atlanta, GA 30361
404-892-2700

625 North Michigan Avenue
Chicago, IL 60611
312-280-0400

1742 Nuuanu Avenue
Honolulu, HI 96817-3294
808-536-2266

First City National Bank Building
Suite 1612
1021 Main Street
Houston, TX 77002
713-652-2977

250 East First Street
Suite 1507
Los Angeles, CA 90011
213-624-8305

299 Park Avenue
Eighteenth Floor
New York, NY 10171
212-371-8222

1830 International Trade Mark
  Building
No. 2 Canal Street
New Orleans, LA 70130
504-529-2101

First Interstate Tower
Suite 2400
1300 S.W. Fifth Avenue
Portland, OR 92701
503-221-1811

1601 Post Street
San Francisco, CA 94115
415-921-8000

Rainier Bank Tower
Suite 3110
1301 Fifth Avenue
Seattle, WA 98101
206-682-9107

Commerce Tower
Suite 2519
911 Main Street
Kansas City, MO 64105-2076
816-471-0111

Federal Reserve Plaza
Fourteenth Floor
600 Atlantic Avenue
Boston, MA 02210
617-973-9772

Japan Information and Cultural
  Center
917 19th Street, N.W.
Washington, D.C. 20006
202-775-0847

Japan Information Center
  299 Park Avenue
  Eighteenth Floor
  New York, NY 10171
  212-371-8222

  845 North Michigan Avenue
  Chicago, IL 60611
  312-321-9560

  1737 Post Street
  San Francisco, CA 94115
  415-921-8000

Embassy of Japan (in Canada)
255 Sussex Drive
Ottawa, Ontario
613-233-6214

Consulates of Japan (in Canada)
  Toronto Dominion Center
  Suite 1803
  P. O. Box 10
  Toronto, Ontario
  416-363-7038

  1155 Dorchester West
    Boulevard
  Suite 2701
  Montreal, Quebec H3B 2K9
  514-866-3429

  730-215 Garry Street
  Credit Union Central Plaza
  Winnipeg, Manitoba R3C 3P3
  204-943-5554

10020 100th Street
Suite 2600
Edmonton, Alberta T5J ON4
403-422-3752

1210-1177 West Hastings Street
Vancouver, British Columbia
   J6E 2K9
   604-684-5868

Ambassade du Japon
7 Avenue Hoche
75008 Paris, France
766-0222

Embassy of Japan
43-46 Grosvenor Street
London W1X OBA England
493-6030

Japanische Botschaft
1006 Berlin-Mitte
Otto-Grotewohl Str.
5/1 Bundesrepublik Deutschland
West Germany
220-2481

Appendix D
Periodicals

Business Japan. Sankei Building, 7-2 Otemachi, 1-chome, Chiyoda-ku, Tokyo 100.

The East. 19-7-101 Minami-Azabu 3, Minato-ku, Tokyo.

The Economic Eye. Keizai Koho Center, Otemachi Building, 6-1 Otemachi, 1-chome, Chiyoda-ku, Tokyo 100.

Industrial News Weekly. Industrial News Agency, 3-10 Kanda Ogawa-cho, Chiyoda-ku, Tokyo 101.

Japan Automotive News. Automotive Herald Company, Ltd., Shinto Building #3, 5-21-5 Shinbashi, Minato-ku, Tokyo 105.

Japan Commerce and Industry. The Japan Chamber of Commerce and Industry, Suite 505, World Trade Center Building, 4-1 Hamamatsu-chome, Minato-ku, Tokyo 105.

The Japan Economic Journal. Nihon Keizai Shimbun, Inc., 1-9-5 Otemachi, Chiyoda-ku, Tokyo 100.

The Japan Industrial & Technological Bulletin. Japan External Trade Organization, Machinery and Technology Department, 2-5 Toranomon, 2-chome, Minato-ku, Tokyo 105.

Japan Letter. P.O. Box 54149, Los Angeles, California 90054, U.S.A.

Japan Petroleum & Energy Weekly. Japan Petroleum Consultants, Ltd., Sanwa Building #3, 4-5-4 Iidabashi, Chiyoda-ku, Tokyo 102.

Japan Publications Guide. Intercontinental Marketing Corporation, IPO Box 5056, Tokyo 100-31.

The Japan Quarterly. Asahi Shimbun, 5-3-2 Tsukiji, Chuo-ku, Tokyo 104.

Japan Steel Journal. Japan Iron & Steel Journal Company, Ltd., Ohki-Sudacho Building, Sixth Floor, 1-23 Kanda, Sudacho, Chiyoda-ku, Tokyo 101.

Journal of Japanese Trade & Industry. Japan Trade & Industry Publicity, Inc., Toranomon Kotohira Kaikan, 2-8 Toranomon, 1-chome, Minato-ku, Tokyo 105.

Look Japan, Ltd. Kawate Building, 2-2 Kanda, Ogawa-cho, Chiyoda-ku, Tokyo 101.

Speaking of Japan. Keizai Koho Center, Otemachi Building, 6-1 Otemachi, 1-chome, Chiyoda-ku, Tokyo 100.

Tokyo Journal. Cross-Culture Jigyodan Company, Ltd., 3-F Magatani Building, 5-10-13 Toranoman, Minato-ku, Tokyo 105.

Tokyo Weekender. Oriental Building, 55-11, Yayoi-cho, 1-chrome, Nakano-ku, Tokyo 164.

Appendix E
Immigration

The types of visas for foreigners in Japan are as follows:

NUMBER	STATUS	LENGTH OF STAY
4-1-1	Diplomats, consular officers, and their suite	Indefinite
4-1-2	Government officials	Indefinite
4-1-3	Transits	15 days
4-1-4	Tourists and temporary visitors for meetings and sporting events	60 days
4-1-5	Commercial business	3 years
4-1-6	Students	1 year
4-1-7	Professors and educators	3 years
4-1-8	Cultural studies	1 year
4-1-9	Entertainers	60 days
4-1-10	Missionaries	3 years
4-1-11	Radio, press, and TV	3 years
4-1-12	Technicians	3 years
4-1-13	Skilled laborers	1 year
4-1-14	Permanent residents	Permanent
4-1-15	Spouse and unmarried children of 4-1-5 through 4-1-13	Same as spouse

NUMBER	STATUS	LENGTH OF STAY
4-1-16 (1)	Temporary residents	180 days
4-1-16 (3)	Special status other than the above (such as spouses of Japanese citizens, children of Japanese mothers, English-conversation teachers)	Up to 3 years

Immigration Offices in Japan

Fukuoka:
1 Okihama-cho
28-7431

Haneda:
Tokyo International Airport
Ota-ku
741-1011

Hiroshima:
4-2 Teppo-cho
21-4411

Kagoshima:
18-2-40 Izumi-cho
22-5658

Kobe:
100-18 Nakayamate-dori, 7-chome
Ikuta-ku
34-7251

Nagoya:
1 Shirakabe-cho, 2-chome
Higashi-ku
941-9561

Osaka:
2 Otamaeno-cho
Higashi-ku
941-0771

Sapporo:
No. 4 West 12, Odori
26-9211

Sendai:
3-3 Gorin, 1-chome
56-6076

Shimonoseki:
2-1 Kamitanaka-machi, 8-chome
23-1431

Takamatsu:
1-10 Nishitakara-cho, 3-chome
61-2555

Tokyo:
3-20 Konan, 3-chome
Minato-ku
471-5111

Yokohama:
51-2 Yamashita-cho
Naka-ku
681-6801

Appendix F
Recommended Reading

General

Christopher, Robert. *The Japanese Mind.* New York: Linden Press, Simon & Schuster, 1983.

Forbis, William H. *Japan Today.* New York: Harper & Row, Publishers, 1975.

Kawasaki, Ichiro. *Japan Unmasked.* Rutland, VT: Tuttle, 1969.

Reischauer, Edwin O. *The Japanese.* Cambridge, MA: Harvard University Press, 1977.

Seward, Jack. *America and Japan: The Twain Meet.* Tokyo: Lotus Press, 1981.

————. *The Japanese.* 11th ed. Tokyo: Lotus Press, 1982.

————. *More about the Japanese.* Rev. ed. Tokyo: Lotus Press, 1983.

Business

Clark, Rodney. *The Japanese Company.* New Haven, CT: Yale University Press, 1979.

Deutsch, Mitchell. *Doing Business with the Japanese.* New York: New American Library, 1983.

Graham, John L., and Yoshihiro Sano. *Smart Bargaining: Doing Business with the Japanese.* Cambridge, MA: Ballinger Publishing, 1984.

Imai, Masaaki. *Never Take Yes for an Answer: An Inside Look at Japanese Business for Foreign Businessmen.* Tokyo: Simul Press, 1975.

JETRO. *Doing Business in Japan.* Tokyo: Gakuseisha Publishing, 1984.

Pascale, Richard Tanner, and Anthony G. Athos. *The Art of Japanese Management: Applications for American Executives.* New York: Warner Books, 1981.

Rohlen, Thomas P. *For Harmony and Strength: Japanese White-Collar Organization in Anthropological Perspective.* Berkeley: University of California Press, 1974.

Yoshino, M.Y. and Litson, Thomas B. *The Invisible Link: Japan's Sogo Sosha and the Organization of Trade.* Cambridge: The MIT Press, 1986.

Cultural

Befu,, Harumi. *Japan: An Anthropological Introduction.* Novato, CA: Chandler Publishing, 1971.

Benedict, Ruth. *The Chrysanthemum and the Sword.* Boston: Houghton Mifflin, 1946.

Keene, Donald. *Appreciations of Japanese Culture.* Tokyo, New York and San Francisco: Kodansha, 1981.

Libra, Takie Sugiyama. *Japanese Patterns of Behavior.* Honolulu: University Press of Hawaii, 1976.

Nakane, Chie. *Japanese Society.* Berkeley: University of California Press, 1970.

Okakura, Kakuzo. *The Book of Tea.* New York: Dover, 1964.

Smith, Robert J. *Japanese Society: Traditions, Self and the Social Order.* New York: Cambridge University Press, 1983.

Suzuki, Shunryu. *Zen Mind, Beginner's Mind.* New York and Tokyo: John Weatherhill, 1970.

Language

Association for Japanese-Language Teaching. *Japanese for Busy People.* Tokyo, New York, San Francisco: Kodansha, 1984.

Editions Berlitz. *Japanese for Travellers.* Lausanne, Switzerland: Editions Berlitz, 1984.

Kershul, Kristine. *Japanese in 10 Minutes a Day.* Seattle: Bilingual Books, 1981.

Mizutani, Osamu, and Nobuko Mizutano, *Nihongo Notes.* Tokyo: The Japan Times, Ltd., 1979.

Nissan Motor Company, Ltd. *Business Japanese.* Tokyo: Bonjin Company, 1984.

Schwarz, Edward A., and Reiko Ezawa. *Japanese Illustrated: Meeting Japan through Her Language.* Tokyo: Shufonotomo Company, 1974.

Umehara, Munetaka. *Japanese Conversation for Travellers.* Tokyo: Kaisosha, 1975.

Glossary

akachochin: literally, red lantern; a pub with a red lantern hanging at its door.

amae: "sweet," indulgent dependence.

anago: eel.

apaato: apartment.

arigato gozaimasu: "thank you very much."

chadai: "tea money"; a gratuity given to the proprietor at an inn.

chotto matte kudasai: "wait a moment, please."

chukai-sha: mediator.

dozo: "please," as in "please come in"; not a request.

dozo yoroshiku: "please feel kindly disposed toward me."

fusuma: sliding door covered with thick paper.

futon: sleeping mattress.

geisha: hostess trained to entertain and to perform in traditional dance and music.

genkan: vestibule.

geta: wooden shoes or slippers

go chiso sama: "it was a feast"; "thanks for the meal."

gomen kudasai: "may I come in, please;" "excuse me."

gomen nasai: "excuse me"; "I'm sorry."

hai: "yes."

hajimemashite: "it's my first time to have the pleasure to meet you."

higan: vernal equinox.

honne: essence.

hoshokin: refundable deposit given to the landlord upon renting an apartment.

iie: "no."

itadakimasu: "I humbly receive"; uttered before starting a meal.

-ji: suffix denoting Buddhist temple.

jinja: Shinto shrine.

ka: group, section.

kacho: section leader, section head.

kangaemasho: "let's think about it."

karaoke: "singing" bar.

katsuo bushi: dried bonito.

kenrikin: "key money"; nonrefundable deposit given to landlord upon renting an apartment; also called *reikin.*

kissaten: coffee shop.

kobun: apprentice.

kohai: junior person.

kotatsu: heating element, formerly of coals, now an electric lamp, under a low table.

kyuri: cucumber.

maguro: tuna.

makizushi: sushi that is rolled in a sheet of seaweed, then sliced.

manshon: expensive apartment.

meishi: business card.

mizu: water.

mizuhiki: cord made of rolled paper, for wrapping gifts.

mizu-wari: "cut" with water, as in "scotch and water."

nomiya: neighborhood pub.

noshi: dried abalone.

o-bon: festival in honor of one's dead ancestors.

o-choko: sake cup.

o-chugen: midsummer festival.

o-kaeshi: gift given in return, in kind.

o-mimai: get-well gift.

onegai shimasu: "please," as in a request.

on-za-roku: "on the rocks," as in "scotch on the rocks."

o-saki ni: phrase uttered when doing anything before someone else.

o-seibo: year-end festival.

o-shibori: small damp towel served before a meal.

o-te-arai: rest room.

o-toshi-dama: New Year's monetary gift.

o-tsukai-mono: gift given as a favor.

oyabun: master, mentor.

rabu hoteru: "love hotel."

reikin: "thank-you money"; nonrefundable deposit given to landlord upon renting an apartment.

rikutsuppoi: too logical, too rational.

ringi: decision by group; shared authority.

ringi-seido: request for group decision.

ringi-sho: written proposal that is circulated first among peers, then upward for senior approval.

ryokan: traditional Japanese inn.

sakazuki: sake cup.

-san: suffix denoting respect, attached to a person's family name; equivalent to "Mr." or "Ms."

sashimi: sliced raw fish.

sempai: senior person.

shacho: president.

shikikin: refundable deposit given to the landlord upon renting an apartment.

shinkansen: "bullet train."

shoji: sliding door covered with paper.

shokai-sha: introducer.

shosha: specialized trading company.

soba: buckwheat noodles.

sogo-shosha: large trading company.

somen: fine noodles.

sopurando: "soapland," euphemism for Turkish bathhouse (see *toruko*).

sumimasen: "excuse me."

sunakku: snack shop.

sushi: raw fish served on small blocks of flavored rice.

tamago: egg.

tatami: rice straw mat.

tatemae: form, external appearance.

teishoku: full meal, as opposed to à la carte.

tera: Buddhist temple.

tokonoma: alcove in a *tatami*-mat room.

toruko: Turkish bath, now called *sopurando.*

tsurekomi hoteru: "love hotel."

udon: wheat noodles.

unagi: eel.

wakarimasen: "I don't understand."

wakarimasu: "I understand."

wasabi: green horseradish.

wa-shoku: Japanese food.

yakitori: grilled chicken.

yoroshiku: "I hope for your continued goodwill."

yo-shoku: Western food.

yukata: cotton robe

zashiki: large *tatami*-mat room.

zen: silent meditation.

Index